# The Author Within
## Bringing Your Message To Life

Sue Kennedy

*All Things Writing*

—— SUE KENNEDY ——

ISBN: 978-0-09896038-4-3
ISBN-13:  9780989603843

Cover layout and design:  Karress Rhodes – KL Graphics

# Table of Contents

# ACKNOWLEDGMENTS

## THANK YOU!!!

I would like to take this time to say a very HUGE thank you to a couple of people that have shaped and helped me to achieve all that I have today. For not long ago I was no where even close to doing what I have been doing in the past 2 years or what I am about to embark on that will completely alter the path of my future, however, it is where I am meant to be and I am really looking forward to this phase of my life.

So please allow me to firstly thank my dear mother who has stood by me through thick and thin, of course she is my mum and what mum wouldn't right? It hasn't been easy for either of us, however she has been my rock and I can't thank her enough.

Next, I would like to thank my very dear friend Julie White. This lady has the most beautiful gift of all and I cannot even begin to explain how grateful I am that our paths crossed once again. Without the help of Julie using the Body Code System on me, I would definitely not be where I am today.

Without the work she did on me with the Body Code System I would never have even dreamt of getting in front of a room full of people speaking let alone doing it with no fear at all. OK, perhaps a couple of little twinges at first!!

I can honestly recommend Julie for those people that have a fear of public speaking. That is just one aspect of what the Body Code can do for you, if you want to live your life in complete happiness, health and wellbeing then please do yourself a favour and give Julie a call on 0448 397 015 or visit her website at www.DevelopBeyond.com.au.

Thank you ladies, love you both to bits xxxooo

# Part One - The Psychology Behind Writing

# Chapter One

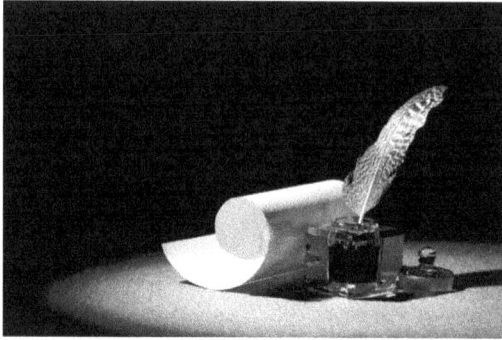

How It All Started

*"To Remain Strong & Focused Will End In Success"*

I love reading and have always had a passion for words. Funny, when I think back to when I was at school, one of my favourite subjects was English! I never in my wildest dreams thought I would become a writer, publish books, and help others with their dreams of writing and publishing their own books.

My English teacher was one of the people that told me I would never amount to much; so glad I didn't take that to heart back then and that I powered on regardless!

After a failed marriage it was time to stand on my own two feet and figure out where life was going to lead me. I answered an ad in the newspaper that was on a course about building your own website and selling affiliate products. The training was quite gruesome and I had to write lots of content for the website, at first I found it quite hard, however, it didn't take me too long before I started to really enjoy this thing called "writing".

Within a few months I had a website built complete with content and products to sell. This was my first taste at building websites and writing. A year went by and my mum was diagnosed with Type 2 Diabetes. The shock of this was insane, we had no history of this in our family, how could this have happened to us?

From this I did hours and hours of research and decided that I needed to have a website so that I could share my findings to help my mum and others that were going through the same situation. This is when my first book was born! I wrote an eBook that is still available today online at www.DefeatDiabetesNow.com.au.

To help promote my eBook, I decided to enter into a writing challenge: 100 articles in 100 days!

Wow, was I crazy or what? I loved each and every moment and by the end of the 100 days I was pumping out 500 to 1000 word articles in 10 minutes! My passion for writing was now set in stone.

I actually decided to get someone else to create my diabetes website so I could concentrate on more research and writing content to load onto my website. This is how I met my business partner, John Flynn. At the time of engaging John to build the website, I never thought that we would then venture into a business together building websites. We had great success working together creating websites for small business owners, however, I decided to follow my passion, which was to write and teach.

In the midst of creating my diabetes website, my marriage fell apart, I lost my beautiful companion, my little Chloe who was a smooth Jack Russell and my home. I fell into a very deep depression and was ready to give up. I am grateful and blessed that I was able to get out of that dark place and move forward, it was very difficult, however, I am here today and so thankful that my life is full of purpose and gratitude and I am surrounded by some very awesome people who remind me each day how beautiful and precious our lives are.

One of the things that did help me get through my depression was to write a book about it. <u>My very first book was written and published.</u> The day it arrived in the post was one of the proudest moments in my life, the feelings it brought up in me to be able to hold a book written by me with my name on it! The feeling is very hard to describe, it was the first time I was truly happy and proud of myself. Of course my mum was quite proud as well!

I not only wrote the book to help myself, it was written with other people in mind, to help them so that they too could move on with a beautifully blessed life like me. The book is called "Anxiety & Depression - Effective Strategies For Coping", it is available from Amazon or my website www.AllThingsWriting.com.au.

From that time on life started to become quite busy and one day I received a phone call asking me if I could run a workshop around online marketing. I'll add you in on a little secret, I was not someone that stood in front of people to speak let alone teach…or so I thought! I accepted the offer, not knowing where to even start. I had quite a few months to prepare the workshop, thank goodness.

While I was thinking about what to teach them, I suddenly thought "wouldn't it be nice to have a book that I could sell at the back of the room".

And with that my next 3 books were born. I started to think about what people would be interested in and what topics people were struggling with. I decided that one of the books should be about helping people know what to do step-by-step in creating their online presence.

The other two topics were on LinkedIn and Google Plus. All three of my books are available on amazon or my websites.

To this day, I still sell my books "at the back of the room" each time I run workshops and they are a huge hit!

**Here's how my new venture "All Things Writing" got up and running:**

As you can see, I have a passion for writing, however, I never really gave it a thought to write for others until one day we built a website for a client, who is also my very dear friend Julie White from Develop Beyond You. Julie wanted me to write the content for her website, so of course I took the challenge and started to write. I sent Julie the draft of her "Meet Julie" page and said to her "wow, this made me cry".

Of course I was very nervous waiting to hear back from Julie, thank goodness she didn't keep me waiting too long! She responded with "Wow, Sue you truly have a gift, where have you been hiding this talent?" You can imagine how I felt. To this day I write for

Julie and love every moment of it.

From that day forward I decided that I should utilise my talents and share it with the world. So "All Things Writing" was created. Apart from writing, I love to teach people and help them succeed in their businesses and life.

**What's next?**

To really give back to people and make sure they do succeed and get the "How to" for everything around writing, I have created workshops, programs and retreats that allow people to get that book within them out onto paper and bring it to life!

Today I share my experiences with others through my workshops, programs, and retreats allowing people to achieve the same success I have gained by showing them how to write successfully step-by-step. To ensure people's success, I also offer one-to-one coaching and mentoring that is a 12-month program that includes my 3-day writer's retreat. I look forward to helping you with your book.

Here's to your writing success!

Sue

# Chapter Two

# The Author Within

*"Writing To Me Is Relaxing & Natural"*

Are you starting to get excited yet? You should be, because in this chapter we are going to uncover that there is a writer within all of us!

Many people talk and think about writing a book and for most that is where it ends...the talking and the thinking. This is where I am going to make sure you realise you will do more than just think and talk about it, we are going to start putting these thoughts onto paper and see where it leads us.

Let me ask you a few questions first, I want you to answer them below or on a bit of paper, whichever, works for you.

• What is your passion?

_____

_____

_____

_____

_____

• What would you like to write about?

_____

_____

_____

_____

_____

• What is your expertise?

_____

_____

_____

_____

_____

• What problems does your audience have?

_____

_____

_____

_____

_____

• What solution can you provide them?

_____

_____

_____

_____

_____

By answering these questions, you can see that you have some wonderful talents within!

It's important to remember these answers will be the basis of what you can write about. The question you need to ask yourself is what type of book would you like to write? There are many different types, and it is important for you to select the one that will work best for you and your circumstances. You need to ask yourself a couple of other questions so that you really know what your purpose is with your book. What is your end goal with the book?

- Is it to promote your business?
- Is it a guideline for your audience?
- Is it full of tips and tricks to help your audience?
- Is it to build credibility for you and your business?
- Will the book be a technical journal?
- Will the book be for children?
- Is it a recipe book?
- Is it a craft book?
- Is it about a hobby?
- Is your book an autobiography?
- Is it a book to give to your clients?
- Is it a book you wish to sell at events or workshops?
- Do you simply want to sell it online?

Now I would like you to pick what the end goal of your book will be:

Please write what that is below:

_____

_____

_____


Next step is to write a couple of paragraphs of what your book is going to be about:

_____

_____

_____

_____

_____

_____

_____

_____

---

---

---

**If you weren't already excited, you should be now!**

You have just taken those talks and thoughts and brought them to life. Congratulations!

So what's the next step? In the next chapter we are going to really drill down and get your chapters and sub topics within each chapter sorted, get ready, this is going to be awesome. You are really going to love how this is done!

However, before we do that, let's take a quick look at your 'why'.

# Your Burning Desire

What is
Your
WHY?

It is really important to understand your 'why'.

Congratulations for taking this exciting step into your future.

Writing your book has the potential to affect your life, your business, your position in the world, and your own personal sense of power. Your book can completely change your life, as you know it.

Before we go any further, let's step into the future and look at how you look as an author…Image a time in the not to distant future when you are holding your book in your hand and seeing your name on an amazing book cover.

I want you to close your eyes for a moment and imagine yourself at the letterbox, taking your package out of the letterbox, you open up the box and there it is…..Your very first book!

You take it out, you hold it, grab it and hold it against your chest for a moment, you then hold it out in front of you, looking at the cover…looking at your name on the front cover of your book, with the biggest smile on your face.

Not only that, imagine the impact your book is going to have on the people that read it. You are communicating an important message; you can see it being purchased by many people and how it affects their lives.

There are only a few things in life that give you as much joy and satisfaction as writing and publishing your own book. This book alongside the writer's retreat that I run will help you achieve this and so much more.

I am going to make sure you get well on your way with your book and the amazing part about all this will be the writer's retreat that will give you all the tools and step-by-step processes to ensure your success!

Now having a vision to write a book is great, but where the rubber meets the road, is by keeping to a consistent schedule so you make solid progress every single day.

The secret to writing a book is consistency.

Your book will not only change your life but the lives of many, just by the impact of your words in your book.

Knowing your 'why' gives you the fuel to write your book and stay consistent no matter the circumstances, you know what's at stake, you know what's in it for you, and that kind of clarity is the first step to writing your book.

Many people never complete their book because they are never clear on their 'why', they don't have the inner drive to complete it and they don't have a connection to their 'big' reason for writing the book in the first place.

Every writer has days where they just want to give up, however, the ones that know their 'why' never do! The 'why' is the carrot dangling in front of you that keeps the words flowing onto the page.

Eventually you will finish your book and your readers will send you thank you wishes letting you know that you have truly accomplished what you first set out to do...have an impact on your readers' lives!

First, start to think about what transformation you want for yourself through writing the book, because many people start writing their book with no real foundations and they become overwhelmed with ideas, hence why the book becomes too hard and so they quit.

This is why the first steps to writing your book are essential and important to understand, focus, concentration and other areas need to be achieved in order to build a strong foundation that will allow you to finish with a strong message.

What is the transformation that you want to accomplish by writing this book?

Let me share with you the transformation I felt once I completed my very first book. Writing my book has completely transformed who I see myself to be in the world. Not only that, I feel very blessed that I can help people with anxiety and depression through my own words and experiences.

This is why it is important to take a look at what it will be like once your book is written, you will see the impact that it has on the world…that is when you have found your 'why'.

**Activity:**

What transformation do you want for yourself from writing your book?

_____

_____

_____

_____

_____

_____

## Unlocking your writing prowess

Like most projects of worthwhile value, writing is no different and needs to be consistent till it gains momentum and results with a tangible outcome. So how do you ensure that there is sufficient motivation to get you going?

The secret lies within you. A believing mind can work wonders to support your mission.

Following are some important questions that you can ask yourself.

1.  List 10 reasons: why I choose to write.

    _____
    _____
    _____
    _____
    _____
    _____
    _____
    _____
    _____
    _____

2.  List 10 outcomes: if I choose <u>NOT</u> to write.

_____

_____

_____

_____

_____

_____

_____

_____

_____

_____

3.  List 10 reasons: why it is important and beneficial
    to share my message with my audience while
    earning a good income from it.

_____

_____

_____

_____

_____

_____

_____

_____

_____

_____

## Activity:

1.  Take 15 minutes each day to do a new list for the above questions. Over time you will experience a clearer understanding of your 'why', and the 'how' will follow without too much difficulty.

2.  If you decide that your writing will not change the world, please do not give up. We are not aiming to make world history with an epic blockbuster, but to provide value to our audiences. Someone in this world right now will benefit from your views, ideas and experiences, if you could only let them out. The internet is just the right platform for finding and sharing your wisdom with your tribe.

3.  Writing styles vary for individuals. If writing a 500 word blog post is not for you, perhaps you will enjoy posting tweets as you go about your day. 'Writing' is a figure of speech here. It is about content sharing, which can extend to audio or video recordings, doodles or photographs.

    Have you got ideas you can share which will benefit others and at the same time earn yourself some income?

List 5 ideas here:

a. I know a lot about

_____ and

will share it by writing blog posts / tweets / audio /
video / webinars / photographs / drawings (fill in
your own).

b. I know a lot about

_____and will

share it by

_____

c. I know a lot about

_____and will

share it by

_____

d. I know a lot about

_____and will

share it by

_____

e. I know a lot about

_____and will

share it by

_____

# Only the Special Accomplish Great Success

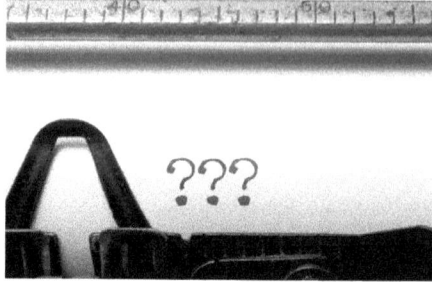

Is writer's block something you suffer from? Some people don't have any problems at all, however, even the best writer's still have an occasional block where they are stuck and not sure how or where to go from that particular point.

Following are some helpful hints to help you with writer's block:

1.  Identify your creative time – is it early a.m., late night, or the middle of the day. That's when to attack your work.

2.  Study what's working and, if possible, what's not working.

3. Research, research, research. Read promotions and immerse yourself in the product, whether it's intellectual (written material) or physical (vitamins, gold coins, air filters, whatever). Google everything that's related to your subject.

4. Identify the "point of maximum anxiety" of your prospect: what keeps your prospect up at night.

5. Identify the USP (unique selling proposition), the big idea of the main promise of your product.

6. Make an outline and begin filling it in.

7. Start ANYWHERE! If you can nail the headline and lead first, great! If not, write anything – the offer, the reply, the back cover, the close (think of the last thing you'd say to someone to get them to buy this book, then start working your way toward that line), sidebars, centerfolds, flyers, bios, premium copy, ANYTHING!

8.  Set some reasonable goals for what you want to achieve each day in your writing.

9.  "Almost cheating": Type the name of the project, the date, and your name in the upper left corner. Then type a page, something like a memo to yourself and other readers. Describe what you see as the core message of what you're about to write. Include a rough idea of how you expect it to look when it's done.

10. "Cheating": Jot down notes and ideas as you prepare. Then transfer them to your computer, typing them up as you go. Guess what? You're already past the "blank page."

11. "Advanced cheating": If you know you always tend to have a problem with empty pages, record your first conversations about your topic or story. You can use a little handheld recorder to do this. Transcribe the recording, and delete any fluff and irrelevant material. Start organising any

useful material into notes and/or sections of your project.

## If you get stuck anywhere along the way

12. Take a break. Run, walk, meditate, go bicycling, listen to music ... then come back to it.

13. If that doesn't work, you need to do more work. Go back to your research and dig some more. Go back to your outline and see if some part doesn't jump out at you as ready to go.

14. Brainstorm with another writer.

If you use these 14 techniques, you should have banished writer's block. If it persists, put your work away and get a good night's sleep. Start fresh in the morning and, in all likelihood, you'll nail it, otherwise, below is another technique that I find very useful.

## Free Writing

A great way to stimulate your creativity and come up with ideas is free writing. This means sitting down with a notebook and scrawling whatever pops into your head. With free writing, you don't worry about whether it's any good or even has a point at all. Just write.
This is an especially good technique for clearing writer's block.

## Why Free Write?

Free writing is a great activity to enhance creativity for a few reasons. One reason is that it trains you to silence your inner critic and just create. It teaches you to let the ideas flow, which is important for any kind of creative activity. It's a kind of drill you can go through to train your mind.

It can also be great for brainstorming ideas. Your free writing may not yield anything you can use. It may just help you get the flow started. But it also might bring forth a great idea. You may hit upon the idea you've been looking for as you 'free associate'. After writing, go back over what you've written and highlight any good ideas you find there.

## How to Free Write

Start by giving yourself a time limit. Set a limit of, for example, ten minutes. Set a timer so that you don't have to pay attention to the time. Start the timer and write. Don't stop writing until the ten minutes is finished. It's a great idea to find a special location or place to write like your bedroom, lounge room, garden etc.

While you're writing, don't edit. Just put the words down and tell yourself you'll go back later. Even typos, misspellings and grammar errors are okay. Even if what you're writing isn't usable, free writing is still serving its purpose by helping to get your idea flow going.

## Coming up Blank

What if you don't know what to write? Especially when you're free writing for the first time, this can happen. You may get stuck wondering where to go next.

When this happens, keep writing the same word or phrase over and over until you're unstuck. As you rewrite the word or phrase, your brain is still working, which means it isn't really stuck at all. Something new will come. Whatever you do, don't stop writing.

Once you get into the habit of free writing, you won't

get stuck so often and more ideas will spring forth.

**Your Free Writing Topic**

Most writers, myself included recommend choosing a topic for your free writing. Write down this topic at the top of the page or find an image on anything and paste that to the top of your page. Don't 'try' to write about it or explain it. Let it be the starting point for your flow of words.

For example, if you're brainstorming a product idea that addresses a problem people have, you can write this problem at the top of your page. Write something like 'weight loss' and then free associate for ten minutes. At best, you'll come up with something in your writing. At least, you'll get yourself started thinking about weight loss.

However, you don't have to have a topic for your free writing. You can simply sit down with the pen, paper and timer, and see where your mind goes. In fact, this is a good way to get started when you're not really sure what to work on. Your mind will naturally draw you into whatever is most interesting to you at the time, or something you're particularly passionate about, or maybe something that's been at the back of your mind. Free writing can be a great self-discovery technique.

## Practice, Practice, Practice

Free writing may seem awkward or strange at first, but it's something that gets better with practice. Devote just five or ten minutes to it each day and you'll see improvements in your creativity. You may even find you can come up with some innovative ideas in just a few minutes that you wouldn't have discovered otherwise.

## Chapter Three

FOCUS
is KEY!

## Setting The Stage

*"One of the main reasons many do not succeed is the lack of focus and concentration"*

Before you begin to write your book, let's discuss Focus and Concentration and how this has an impact not only on your life, but also on writing your masterpiece!

According to research by the National Center for Biotechnology Information of the National Library of Medicine, the average attention span in the year 2000 was 12 seconds. By 2015, it has shrunk to 8.25.

Are you still with me? Please, take your nose out of your smartphone for just a moment more...

We often joke about how electronic devices and instant

internet gratification have shortened our attention spans to that of small furry mammals, but what the above statistic shows is that this is no joke at all.

We are increasingly logging in to our social media accounts and then forgetting what it was we were going to do there and instead start watching a video of a teenager in Wisconsin's dramatic backyard do a face-plant or a kitten in Australia do a yoga routine.

The other really important part of this aspect is to understand that there are two types of people, and they are:

**Through time people:** Being a 'through time' person is to be conscious of time passing, to be aware of the interaction of events, time to attend a meeting approaching. It is also to be able to plan, and work to a plan, and to complete.

**In time people:** Being an 'in time' person you are less likely to be aware of time passing, less likely to plan or stick to a plan and can become side-tracked.

Understanding which 'time' type you are will help you achieve success a lot easier.

Following are some guidelines to help you with focus and concentration.

## Where is the Noise Coming From?

What are your main distractions? It may seem simple enough to identify them and they're usually related to technology. But for the purposes of really uncovering the distractors that hound you, we'll need to make a slightly deeper analysis. In addition, not all distractions are of a technological nature. Let's take a broader view.

Research into distractions, which refers to them as 'noise', identifies two broad categories – external interference and internal interference.

## Tips and Techniques to Improve your Focus at Work

Learning how to improve your concentration and focus is nothing more than mastering a few techniques, or making a few lifestyle changes. Sometimes, it just takes forming a new habit and you'll see results immediately.

You probably know many of the techniques already. They're methods most people know, but we fail to implement them. Sometimes, this is simply because we don't understand just how important they can be in boosting focus and concentration.

You'll see some techniques you're already using and find a few that you can easily implement in your daily life. First, we'll look at tricks and healthy habits, and then ways to get organised for better focus and time management techniques. Use this as a toolbox of techniques and choose those that are most feasible and effective for you.

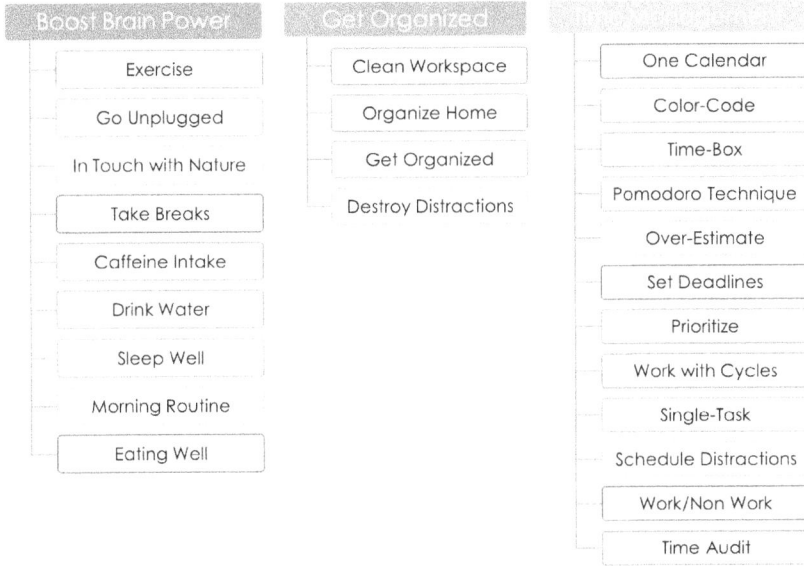

| Boost Brain Power | Get Organized | |
|---|---|---|
| Exercise | Clean Workspace | One Calendar |
| Go Unplugged | Organize Home | Color-Code |
| In Touch with Nature | Get Organized | Time-Box |
| Take Breaks | Destroy Distractions | Pomodoro Technique |
| Caffeine Intake | | Over-Estimate |
| Drink Water | | Set Deadlines |
| Sleep Well | | Prioritize |
| Morning Routine | | Work with Cycles |
| Eating Well | | Single-Task |
| | | Schedule Distractions |
| | | Work/Non Work |
| | | Time Audit |

## Exercises to Improve your Focus and Concentration

In addition to getting organised and learning new habits, there are other beneficial exercises that you can perform daily to help you improve focus and concentration. The exercises below are all easy to practice. You don't need to spend a great deal of time on these exercises. Something like 5-10 minutes per day is enough to produce results (although more doesn't hurt).

These exercises include:

- Mindful meditation
- Noting distractions
- Mantra techniques
- Deep breathing
- Visualisation
- Ambient sound meditation
- Music for focus
- Memorise something
- Don't move
- Counting backwards
- Fix your gaze
- Switch hands
- Do puzzles or colouring in for adults
- Mindful work
- Learn a language

## Create your Focus and Concentration Action Plan

Now, it's time to put everything together and create an action plan that you can use to begin improving your concentration and focus.

Start by reviewing the tips on "Tips and Techniques to Improve Focus at Work." Then, go over the learning activity from above and look at the exercises you've chosen to try. Now, answer the following questions.

## Health and Nutrition:

1. How can you add 15 to 20 minutes of physical activity into your day? Be as specific as possible (For example, walk to the train station and back during morning break at work).
2. How many glasses of water do you drink each day? How can you get a few more glasses in?
3. How many cups of coffee or other caffeinated beverages do you drink in a day? How many would you like to be drinking and at what times (For example, two cups in the morning)?
4. How many hours of sleep do you need in order to function at your best? What steps can you take to ensure that you get that sleep?
5. What is your morning routine? If you don't have one, what would you like your morning routine to be like?
6. Do you eat breakfast every day? If not, how can you make it easy for yourself to get the nutrition you need before you start your day?

Based on your responses to the above questions, create a daily schedule that maps out:

- Your morning routine
- Breakfast
- Food and beverage intake throughout the day
- Exercise and other breaks
- Bed time (including a bedtime ritual if you need help sleeping)

Make several copies of your answers and put them in places where they can be used as reminders, such as by the bed, on your fridge, your desk at work, and so on. The goal is to create new habits that become second nature over time. When the time comes, you can get rid of the reminders, but for now, keep them around so you remember and don't cheat.

## Getting Organised:

1. Pick a day in the next week to organise your workspace. This includes your desk, walls, paper files, and digital files. Clean and organise everything.
2. Decide on times throughout the day and set times during the week for regular tidying up. Put a big clean up on your calendar once a month.
3. Choose a method for de-cluttering your house and continuing this theme choose specific days on next month's calendar for de-cluttering. A good way to do this is to set aside a different day for different areas of the house.
4. Go through the techniques to reduce distractions and create a plan that incorporates them. Try starting with just one tip at a time. Master that one tip and then move on to the next. Wherever possible, set deadlines and put things on your calendar.

## Time Management:

1. If you are using multiple calendars, integrate them into one. Choose colours for identifying key categories.
2. Front-load your schedule so that you get more done earlier.
3. Consider using time boxes for daily tasks.
4. Break large projects into small goals and steps that you can attach a deadline to.
5. Make sure that you're single tasking and not multi-tasking.
6. Try the Pomodoro (kitchen timer) technique one day this week and see if it works for you.
7. Consider performing a time audit.

## Mindfulness:

1. Take your newly created calendar and add a daily mindfulness activity. Start by scheduling 5-10 minutes, 2-3 times per week. Eventually, move it to five days a week.
2. For some great mindfulness resources, please take a look at http://www.mindfulnesscds.com/

## Conclusion and Next Steps

Achieving and sustaining focus is harder in today's complex and technologically driven world than ever before. The technologies that distract us and divert our attention aren't going anywhere. In fact, it's a situation that will likely deepen as our lives become more entwined with technology.

It's hard to maintain focus, but it's really just a matter of learning techniques, habits and exercises to help you concentrate, as well as gaining the self-awareness to understand when and how you are distracted. This is where the mindfulness exercise is very useful.

For a complete understanding of Focus and Concentration, my workshop called "Laser Focus" is a great way to help you succeed in this area. The link to this workshop is: www.allthingswriting.com.au/online-training-programs.

# Chapter Four

# Expressing Your Thoughts

*"There is no greater inspiration than to put your thoughts into words that you can share'*

Writing your book is all about expressing your thoughts, getting your message out to the world and of course sharing your own experiences with others.

Writing a book about what you know in business or your own life experience is a known way to establish credibility and instant authority about a subject. If you have achieved business or technical acumen while working at your job or career, you have the basis of a good book that can help others in their journeys.

You'll be able to establish your own credibility and sell books while your own business efforts soar in popularity because this way you establish being a well-earned authority in your market.

Writing a book is likely the most challenging task you can undertake, but it also brings with it many rewards. It doesn't take talent as much as it takes persistence and patience. So, sharpen your pencils and get ready to begin. By the end of this book, you'll have everything you need to write your own book.

## What to Write About

If you're thinking about writing a book, you probably already have a concept in mind. You may have an area of expertise that relates to your business or your personal life that many people would be interested to know about.

An idea doesn't have to be about your business. It may be about a hobby or an idea you have that could change the world – or at least make life easier for someone. The concept for your book can take many forms, but whatever form it takes, you should immerse yourself in it as much as you can when you decide on the topic.

The first step is to gather information about all your ideas before you begin the writing process.

Research is important to developing your concept. You'll get many ideas from your research, condensing and formulating your ideas to fit your specific audience is key. You're way ahead if you're planning to write about something you already know, but it still takes research to fill in the blanks about what you don't know and to make the book flow easily.

**Brainstorm Book Ideas**

Even if you're thinking about writing a book about your expertise, you may not know how to structure it or which audience is the best for your knowledge and style of writing.

Your best writing will be when you are interested in the topic, so make sure you choose something that really appeals to you. When you are writing your book, this interest and excitement is what will keep your audience interested and reading till the end.

Following are some ideas that can help you with your brainstorming:

- **Your Job** – Even an ordinary job can produce a myriad of ideas.
- **Experience** – Many people have made millions from chronicling their experiences. Some of the best-known books have been ones that involved those who worked near an influential person, leader or celebrity. These are often called "tell all" books. Of course, not everyone has an experience like that. Perhaps you would like to

talk about what happened when you hiked through Europe or about rescuing dogs.

- **Passion** – If you've had a passion that has been a big part of your life for quite some time, you may have the basis for a book idea. You may have a passion for the business that you've built and developed online or offline. Telling others about your experience each step of the way is a good concept for a book that people who have the same or similar passion will want to read.
- **Hobby** – Whatever hobby you have is definitely sure to be shared by others. You may have turned a hobby into a lucrative business – that's fascinating stuff for some people and you might be an inspiration to others if you write a book about your experience.

  New opportunities always arise as times and technologies evolve, so there will always be a book you can write to fill that need. Brainstorming your ideas of expertise and experiences will help you write your book.

Following are a few brainstorming methods to help you:

- **Random Input Method** - the random input method is a very creative way to brainstorm that triggers the imagination. It involves taking some random input from somewhere that's not related to the topic of your brainstorming, and using this random thing to inspire ideas.

The random input could be a word, a picture, a sound, or anything else that opens new lines of thinking. You make associations with your topic and the new input, or make associations between different random inputs, and come up with new ideas.

The random input isn't some kind of oracle that magically gives you the answer. Rather, it's a form of outside stimulus that gets you to think differently and thus come up with new ideas.

There's an often-told legend that Campbell's Soup used the random input method to come up with its Chunky Soup. Supposedly, they were brainstorming using a random word tool. The tool gave them the word "apartment," which they then free associated, coming up with a stream of words that went something like this: "apartment," "build," "tools," "hammer," "saw," "drill" and so on. It eventually led to the word "fork," which led someone to say, "What if you could eat soup with a fork?" Another participant responded that it would have to be chunky.

There are many ways to find random input you can use for your brainstorming. A few ideas include:

- Flipping open a dictionary to a random word
- Putting a random word or phrase into Google or Google's image search
- Turning on the TV or radio and using what's on
- Pulling a random book, CD or DVD off the shelf
- Picking a random object from somewhere in the room
- Looking outside your window and using the first thing you see or the first thing that passes by

Be creative with what you find and freely associate, as the brainstormers at Campbell's Soup did.

## Activity - Random Input

1. Choose one of the ideas from your previous brainstorming for a random input and,
2. Try the random input method with a group or with a friend.

| Ideas from Random Input | Notes |
|---|---|
| | |
| | |
| | |
| | |
| | |
| | |
| | |

| Top Three Ideas |
|---|
| |
| |
| |

- **New Perspective Method** - With the new perspective method, you take the problem and consider it from another perspective. There are a variety of different ways you can do this. You could take another person's point of view. For example, try considering the issue from the point of view of your customers, or someone in another country.

You can choose a famous person, public figure or person from history and try to consider the problem from their point of view. How would Steve Jobs deal with your human resources problem, or what kind of branding concept would Socrates come up with?

Instead of a different person, try seeing the problem from a different era in time. Take your modern business problem back to Ancient Rome or Medieval Japan.

Your new perspective could be another part of the world or another industry. For example, how would an airplane mechanic or a circus performer handle the problem?

If you're brainstorming in a group setting, you could assign a different perspective to each member. Assign your sales team the roles of Mark Twain, Confucius, Joan of Arc and Charlemagne. You can do the same with eras in history, parts of the world, industries, etc.

One particular technique that uses the new perspective approach is what's called the Six Thinking Hats. It involves putting on six different hats to consider the problem using different perspectives. The hats are:

**White** – This is the factual hat that just considers the information available, or what facts are known about the problem.

**Black** – The black hat is the risk-averse hat, which considers the problem from the point of view of all that could go wrong. It places security as the top priority.

**Yellow** – This is the hat of optimism, which explores the positives to the black hat's negatives. It looks at benefits and seeks harmony.

**Green** – The green hat is the creativity hat, which considers alternatives and other possibilities.

**Red** – The red hat is the intuitive hat. It bases decisions on emotions and gut instincts.

**Blue** – The blue hat is the management hat, which makes sure that each hat acts in accordance with its role and makes sure the brainstorming session stays on track.

## Activity – New Perspective

1. Try the new perspective method in a brainstorming session for a specific problem  you need to address.
2. Try the Six Thinking Hats in a brainstorming session or to evaluate the ideas generated in a brainstorming session.

| Ideas from Perspective/6 Hats | Notes |
|---|---|
|  |  |
|  |  |
|  |  |
|  |  |
|  |  |
|  |  |
|  |  |

| Top Three Ideas |
|---|
|  |
|  |
|  |

- **Speed Thinking Method** - Speed thinking is basically brainstorming ratcheted up a notch. Whenever brainstorming, it's always good to time your sessions and get as many ideas down as possible. Speed thinking does the same thing but takes it a step further by imposing tight time limits and putting on a bit more pressure.

There is a variety of speed thinking techniques but all involve setting a time limit and giving participants a goal. An example might be something like 20 ideas in 2 minutes. It puts the pressure on the participants to come up with as many ideas as they can. You can create other rules and parameters to gamify it and increase your efficiency.

Speed thinking works best in short bursts of thinking with short breaks in between. You can combine speed thinking with other methods. For example, you can assume roles for a speed brainstorming session, and then take a break and switch roles. You can set a time limit and idea goal for free associations from random input.

One speed thinking variation is what's called 6-3-5 Brain writing (also called Method 635 or the 635 Method), developed by marketer Bernd Rohrbach. The method involves six participants who each have to write down three ideas on their sheets individually within five minutes. The ideas can be expressed as words or as images or symbols. At five minutes, the sheets are passed to the participant on the right. At the end of 30 minutes, you have a total of 108 ideas.

You can actually perform 6-3-5 Brain writing with any number of participants. More participants would produce more ideas, but with more than about seven it starts to get unwieldy. This also makes the overall session longer.

## Activity – Speed Thinking

1. Try a few quick speed-thinking sessions, preferably with a group.
2. Try 6-3-5 Brain writing or a variation of it.

| Ideas from Speed Thinking | Notes |
|---|---|
|  |  |
|  |  |
|  |  |
|  |  |
|  |  |
|  |  |

| Top Three Ideas |
|---|
|  |
|  |
|  |

- **The Stepladder Technique Method** - The stepladder technique can only be used in a group setting. However, it harnesses the power of both individual and group brainstorming.

First, a topic or problem is presented to all of the people within the group. Every person except for two leaves the room. The two that remain in the room brainstorm together on the problem. Each other person brainstorms by himself or herself individually.

The two remaining in the room hold their brainstorming session for a set period of time. At the end of this time, the first of the other people is called back into the room. This person shares the ideas they came up with in isolation with the two who have already been brainstorming.

All three continue their discussion together for a set period of time and then the next person is called into the room. Each person is called back into the room one by one to add their ideas to the discussion.

The reason that the stepladder technique works so well is that each person gets to express his or her own individual ideas. It gets everyone involved equally. It also prevents groupthink, where people go along with the ideas of others instead of coming up with their own, and other common problems that can occur in-group brainstorming sessions.

# Activity – The Stepladder Technique

1. Try the stepladder technique at your next group brainstorming session.

| Ideas from Stepladder | Notes |
|---|---|
|  |  |
|  |  |
|  |  |
|  |  |
|  |  |
|  |  |
|  |  |

| Top Three Ideas |
|---|
|  |
|  |
|  |

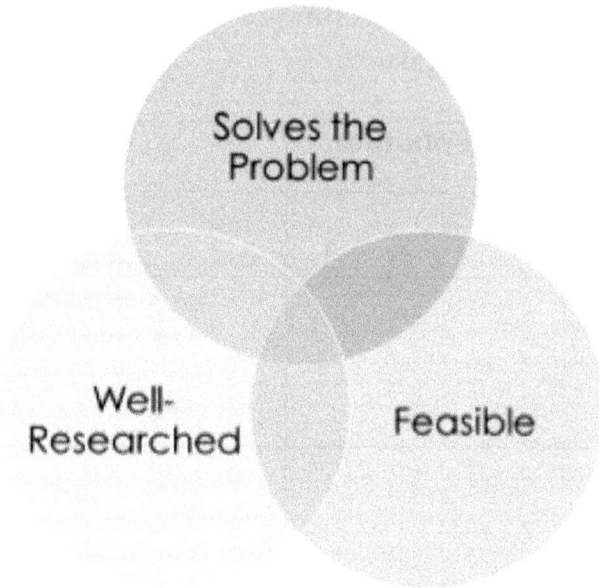

**Researching Your Book**

No matter how much you think you know about the subject you're going to write about, you'll need to do some heavy and meaningful research before you sit down to write.

Now that we have the internet, there are many ways to research a subject, however, you don't have to use the "search" button exclusively for all your research needs. Following are some methods you may not have thought of to research for your book:

- **Libraries** – Your local library or university libraries are great places to search for information. The archives of some libraries may have information that you can't easily find on the internet. However, you can use the outstanding databases within the library to locate what you need.

- **Books and Magazines** – Local bookstores (and those online) likely harbour a wealth of information about the subject you want to write about. You might find some great ideas and new information in monthly magazines and many books that present a different slant on your chosen subject.

- **Interviews** – When you're writing a non-fiction book, it's especially helpful to have interviews or quotes from experts other than yourself. You may also be able to clarify some of your own thoughts on a subject. Interviews and quotes from others give your book much more credibility.

- **Blogs** – There is a blog site for just about any subject that you can think of. Blogs on the internet are great places to learn new things and get ideas. It's a way for people all over the world, with the same interests, to get together and talk about what they love.

- **Social Media Sites** – You may think these sites are frivolous and won't do you much good when researching your book. But, just as there are blog sites about many subjects, there are also groups on social media sites who boast members with the same interests. Find and join one that might provide some insight into your subject.
- **Government Agencies** – The government distributes thousands of documents about thousands of subjects. If you're writing a book that might need research involving rules and regulations set forth by the government, these agencies might be just the place to do some research.

One main rule of thumb you should remember when collecting your research data is to be sure – very sure – that your information is factual. Nothing turns off a reader than to come across a blatant error in a book. The author and the book immediately lose all the credibility they may have built.

## Stories That Sell

Research shows that likeability is one of the main drivers behind consumer purchase decisions. There are many ways to make yourself 'likeable', however a good story about yourself or your brand is one of the most effective and memorable ways to do it. The likeability of a good story has a bigger influence on your customer than anything else.

Stories engage a number of parts of the brain. In addition to areas dealing with language and logic, they also activate areas related to sensory stimuli. A study by the Emory Institute in Atlanta in which participants read the novel Pompeii and then had MRI scans found that the novel's story led to increased activity in the left temporal cortex, which is one area highly associated with language. It also found that just thinking about an action triggers the same areas that performing the action does.

Gregory Berns, the lead author of the study, said, "The neural changes that we found associated with physical sensation and movement systems suggest that reading a novel can transport you into the body of the protagonist."

Compare this to what the brain does when it takes in facts and data. When looking at data, the language areas of the brain light up, but not the emotional and sensory areas. These are triggered only by stories. This means that your story engages your audience in ways data can't. In addition to thinking, they're feeling and actually experiencing the story.

People forget statistics and facts, but they don't forget a good story.

This is especially true if your story conveys a message related to things your audience cares about deeply. According to Jennifer Aaker, Professor of Marketing at Stanford Graduate School of Business, "Stories are 22 times more memorable than facts alone." Further, she says, "Studies show that we are wired to remember stories much more than data, facts, and figures. However, when data and story are used together, audiences are moved both emotionally and intellectually."

Stories are memorable not only because of the emotional connection but also because they stand out. Amid all of the content clutter of the internet, a story gets attention. Think for a minute of the many articles you can find online that offer X number of tips for doing something. They're all fairly generic. But what if you found a compelling story that ends with a list of takeaway tips? That's something you'd be more likely to pay attention to.

Because of the explosive growth of social media and content marketing, stories are more important and effective than ever. Online, we're not broadcasting advertising messages as we did through traditional media like TV and print. Effective online marketing doesn't sell, it informs and entertains. After consuming your content, your audience naturally thinks of you when they need your products or services. Stories offer an even better way to do this.

Your stories create an emotional connection between your target market and your product or brand. They have a psychological effect that adds tremendous power to your marketing and the ultimate growth of your business.

While you may think that good storytelling is only for people with a born ability, there are tricks and processes that will make it easy for anyone.

There are different story formats and elements of a good story, but first, let's see what kinds of stories you can tell.

## The Company / Brand Story

This is the story of your company or brand. Stories are very important for your brand because they contribute so much to your brand's image. A company story usually involves how the company came into existence and grew to its current state, often told personally by the founder or first employees. Through the company's story, you convey to your audience the values and culture of your company. It also offers many opportunities for you to include the formats we'll discuss later (rags to riches, conquering the monster, etc.).

A good example of a brand story is the story of Nike's waffle-tread shoes. The story says that Nike founder Bill Bowerman one day, in a fit of inspiration, poured rubber into a waffle iron, thus giving birth to the waffle-tread. What this story tells you about the company is that it's innovative and not afraid to try out crazy ideas that could possibly revolutionise shoes, as we know them.

## The Personal Story

A personal story is a story from someone's life. It could be how they overcame difficulties or how they reached the place where they are today. It could be something as simple as a scene the writer observed a few days ago that has relevance to their topic and their audience.

Many personal stories involve overcoming difficulties. For example, you might write a story about a time when you couldn't manage your time well. You were always busy and had many things to do, but no free time to do what you enjoyed. This is the setting of the story. You then discovered a very simple and handy technique for managing time better, which helped you get more done and have more time to yourself.

## The Product Story

You can tell stories that relate to products. Your story could be how the product was developed, why it came into existence, a problem the product makers had to solve, or how a customer used it in a creative way.

A good example of a product development story is the one about the origin of the idea for the Sony Walkman. It started with a Sony executive who liked to listen to classical music on his long flights overseas. However, he hated dragging around a cassette player. He asked his engineers to create something smaller and more portable – and the Walkman was born. This is what gave us not only the Walkman, but also, by extension, all of the pocket-sized portable music players we enjoy today.

One way to discover great product stories is to ask your customers to write the stories for you. This is an example of what's called 'crowdsourcing', in which you turn some part of your content creation over to your audience. Crowdsourcing is a highly effective content marketing strategy because it gets your audience actively engaged.

An example of crowd-sourced content is Patagonia's Worn Wear campaign. Outdoor clothing designer Patagonia asked its customers to send in their stories of the adventures they experienced wearing Patagonia's clothes. People sent in their stories and these stories were featured online and in YouTube videos.

**The Customer Story**

A customer story is one in which your customer relates somehow to your product or service. This is one of the best types of stories because it emphasises the benefits of your offerings. When people read about a customer's own experience with your product or service, they can put themselves in the customer's place and understand directly how your products or services can benefit them. These stories are also great because they're authentic.

A customer story can focus on a common problem your market faces and how one particular customer overcame this problem with your product. For example, if you sell an office filing system, you could ask customers to send in their stories about how their work is different after they started using your system. Even better, ask them to send in pictures of their newly organised files so that you can illustrate the stories.

## The Employee Story

Employee stories are engaging because they take people behind the scenes and add a human element to your company. Your audience gets a glimpse of the inner workings of your company and how every person involved makes a difference. These stories also help to convey your corporate culture.

An employee story might feature a particular employee and how they've improved a product or service, helped the company reach one of its goals, or bent over backwards for a customer in need. It might also be their own history of how and why they came to the company. An employee story is something personal or professional about someone who works for your company and which you feel will resonate with your audience.

## The Case Study

A case study is a more detailed and researched story of a person, group, activity, event, problem, and so on. The case study comes from the social sciences but companies also use it for exploring potential problems or situations. One type is the historical case study, which can be used in a similar way to your company story.

The main difference between a case study and the other story types we discussed is the thoroughness of it. A case study includes a great deal of research and organisation in order to present every aspect of it. A case study might look something like a detailed retelling of your company's history or the development of a product.

A good story is one that engages the audience. In addition to the story lines we discussed earlier, your story also has to have certain elements that make it engaging. We covered some of this previously as we discussed story examples, but here are the elements that make any good story engaging.

## Emotional Connection

As mentioned before, a good story is one that makes an emotional connection. Compassion gets donors to give money. Concern gets consumers to beef up their PC security software. A sense of mystery and discovery drives quest stories and loathing of the terrible monster adds suspense and excitement to conquering the monster stories.

Your story should be genuine and from the heart, and connect with your audience's pain points, values and desires.

## Relatable Characters

Stories have little effect if we don't relate to their characters. Just think back to any TV show you watched or book you read where you didn't really care whether the characters lived or died. It wasn't very compelling, was it?

When we can relate to the characters in your story, it keeps us engaged. We're cheering for the hero and hoping that she'll win. We hope the hero returns home, conquers the monster, bounces back from their huge setback, or reaches their journey's end.

In order to create stories with compelling characters,

use people who reflect the values of your market. Choose characters your audience can identify with, the people who will make them say, "That guy or girl is just like me, or like someone I know." Whenever possible, use real customers and real employees.

## Suspense and Anxiety

Suspense and anxiety are important elements in any story. They keep the audience glued to the story to see what will happen in the end. Although everybody knows that James Bond won't get killed by the villain an hour into the movie, we're still on the edge of our seats as we watch the drill get closer to his head. Suspense and anxiety are more powerful in storytelling than the rational mind, which says, "That wouldn't happen."

## Inspiration

Stories don't have to be inspirational to be interesting (remember the tragedy storyline). When it comes to telling stories in a marketing context, you want to inspire the audience. A fundraising ad that shows starving children isn't meant to drive you to despair and give up hope. They always say, "You can make a difference."

Inspiration is important in a marketing context because it influences the person to take action. Taking action could mean buying a product, or it could be something more subtle such as aligning yourself with a brand and its vision. Stories that don't offer this hope and inspiration don't usually lead the audience to take action.

## The Structure of a Good Story

Samuel Beckett's absurdist play "Waiting for Godot" has been hailed as one of the most important plays of the 20th Century. The main story line is about two men waiting around for a man named Godot who, by the closing of the second act, never arrives. To summarise, nothing much really happens.

While it would be ignorant to say that one of the greatest plays of the 20th Century doesn't have a "good" story line, this is not the kind of story you'd want to tell in a marketing context. "Waiting for Godot" is an experimental play and the story is harder to discern than that of a traditional story. For our purposes here, you want your stories to be direct and obvious for the most impact possible.

A well-structured story has a clear beginning, middle and end. The classic story is based around conflict and that conflict's resolution. The conflict is what keeps us tuned in and engaged. It provides suspense and anxiety to move the story along. Even though we know it will turn out well for our characters, the resolution of the conflict (called the "climax") at the end gives us a sense of release and triggers positive emotions.

Let's take for our example the film "The Goonies." In "The Goonies," a group of ragtag kids go off in search of One-Eyed Willie's hidden treasure in order to save their home from foreclosure. All the while, scary yet buffoonish gangsters pursue them.

The gangsters chase the kids who have trouble finding the treasure, nearly giving up at one point; we feel the suspense and anxiety. The story is resolved when they finally find the treasure, the gangsters are arrested, and the family is able to pay off the foreclosure.

Even though an ad or story for marketing may be very short, it still includes these elements. Let's take for an example, the Red Bull ad that features Felix Baumgartner's record-breaking free-fall from 128,000 feet.

The conflict is that he has to jump from what is basically outer space and land safely back on earth. Logically, you know that if he had burst into flames upon reentry or if his parachute had failed, Red Bull probably wouldn't have chosen to tell the story. But still, when you see him perched on the edge of the capsule surrounded by the black reaches of outer space, you feel the pinch of anxiety. Then, once you see the people cheering and his safe landing, you get a feeling of relief and elation as the conflict resolves.

Here are a few other tips on creating engaging stories:

## The Product Is Secondary

In all good marketing stories, the product is in the background. When telling a story, focus on making it a good story, not on promoting the brand or product. Just like other forms of content marketing, your story will do the selling for you.

If you're telling a product story, of course the product will take center stage. Its benefits will be a major part of the story. But remember that it doesn't have to be, and in general, the less promoting the better.

To use the Felix Baumgartner story as an example, you'll notice that you don't see Baumgartner emerge from under the parachute to swig a Red Bull and gasp, "Ahhh!" And as far as I know, there aren't any interviews with him where he says that he simply wouldn't have had the energy to do the jump if not for the taurine and glucuronolactone in Red Bull.

## Show the Benefits

The best stories reflect the benefits of the product without actually saying it. The viewer makes a connection in their mind, and the connection is much stronger when it's made this way.

## Part of a Bigger Story

Another good story element is to make the story you're telling part of a much bigger story. It helps to advance the concept or idea behind the brand or product. If you think back to Nike's waffle iron story, it ostensibly tells you the story of how Nike's founder created the waffle pattern. But what the story really says is, "Nike is a company that innovates and changes the world."

## Use Your Brand Personality

In whatever story you tell, your brand personality should play a major part. It makes sense for Red Bull to tell the story of Felix Baumgartner's jump since its brand personality is associated with extreme sports. Let your brand personality come through.

## Break up the Story

One effective storytelling technique is to break up the story. Instead of telling the entire story all at once, offer just one scene or part of it. This is a good way to keep your audience tuned in for the next installment. This is where you end your advertisement with "to be continued…"

## Story within a Story

Another idea is to create stories within a story. An example of this from literature is the One Thousand and One Nights, commonly called "Arabian Nights." Each story in the collection ties in to the entire collection. This is what you're doing when you create a number of short stories that all follow a similar theme or topic. Tell your story without giving it all away so people will tune in to the next installment

## Make Stories Share-worthy

When you look at all of the content that gets widely shared or goes viral, it has one thing in common – it sparks strong emotions. These stories are awe-inspiring, amusing, moving, illuminating, inspiring, shocking, cute, sexy, scary, infuriating or controversial. Spicing your stories up with these emotions will help your stories get shared, but make sure they're appropriate for your brand and audience.

## Make Visual Stories

A picture, and by extension a video, says a thousand words. This is no exaggeration. The more visual elements you can add into your story, the more likely it will be shared. In fact, you can create images that tell stories without actually saying anything at all. The reason visual elements make stories more effective is that they directly trigger more emotions.

For a more comprehensive look into how storytelling can help you, take a look at my **detailed step-by-step workshop.**

Available at www. allthingswriting.com.au/online-training-programs

# Chapter Five

# Who is your audience?

*"There's no point writing your book if your audience is not interested"*

Every business needs a target market to focus on and market to effectively. The most important part of any business is knowing who your target audience is, without knowing who that is how can you possibly sell your products or services. It does not matter if you are in business or not, or you are writing your book, you still need to know who your audience is. What if there is no audience, do think you will sell anything? The answer of course is 'no'.

Before you start to market your product or service you MUST know who your audience is, otherwise you might as well forget it, you will not be successful.

Let me give you an example, if you had a product that was for dogs and the people you were marketing to only liked cats, they will not be interested at all, and they definitely will not buy!

There are people out there that want and need your product or service, so the goal of your marketing is to connect with them. By knowing clearly who that target market is, you can be sure that your efforts will be successful. Otherwise you are just going to stumble across someone that might be interested or go in a completely wrong direction, like I mentioned about the dogs and cats!

### What is a Target Market?

A target market is a clearly defined group of people for you to direct your marketing efforts to. They are a specific audience. Your target market is defined by demographics like age, gender, location, economic group, social status, family situation, country and language. Following are a few examples of target markets:

- A resort that targets retirees
- A store that targets young families
- A shopping network that targets working mums over 30

- A clothing store that targets teenagers who see themselves as 'alternative'

As you can see, not all the information above is related to demographics. For example, the teenagers that see themselves as 'alternative'. There are other factors to consider, like psychographic data, like how your target audience views themselves in the world around them. This can be just as important as the demographic information.

## Why Laser-Target Your Market?

In marketing, you either hit or miss there is no in-between, defining your market gives you somewhere to aim. Therefore, if you don't target your market perfectly, you will waste not only your time, but your money as well when you are sending your message to the wrong people.

A perfect example of this would be:

Running an ad for your retirees at the resort that showed a video or picture of teenagers dancing wildly to loud punk rock music, this would be very ineffective.

The key to successful marketing is to identify your market's problem and then provide them with the solution they are looking for.

Once you know exactly who they are, you can communicate your product or service benefits and the results they can expect in a language that they can understand. An example of this would be telling your target market of retirees that at the resort, they will not have to compete with the crowds and you can tell your alternative teenagers that they don't need to fit in with the latest fads.

The benefit of this is that your target market can relate to each other. By identifying them and marketing to them, you can create a 'tribe' based around common interests. This can be especially powerful online, where people spend a great deal of time on social networking sites, forums, and blogs.

When defining your target market, never make assumptions. Listen to what your target market says and base your marketing and writing decisions on that data. Do surveys to find out exactly what they want!

**Your Target Market Profile**

Market research helps you create a profile of your perfect customer so that you can formulate your business strategies with precision.

The goal of your market research is to create a profile of one individual who is your perfect customer, your avatar. This profile has to be as complete as possible. It should include not only demographic and geographic information, but also how they feel about things. Psychographic information includes things like how people in your market see themselves, how they use your products or services, what they are most afraid of, what they hope for in the future, and other information.

In order to gather this information, you need to analyse hard data about your audience.

There are two types of data - quantitative and qualitative. Both of these are essential in creating an accurate picture of your target market.

The quantitative research looks at the big picture. It takes a large sample of over a hundred people or more and uses that same sample to look at trends. If you were to pick one hundred random people in your market, you can probably assume that they would represent the general population of your market.

The traditional and most common method of quantitative research is to do a survey. With your survey, you can discover that 70% of the sample audience finds your new product attractive. From that you could then assume that 70% of all consumers would think that as well.

Qualitative research is a bit more tricky, however, it yields some important data that you will not get through your quantitative methods of research. It does not deal in numbers but in words, images, impressions, and feelings. This is a more in-depth and objective approach where you can interact with your sample audience.

The most common qualitative method is a focus group. An example of this is where you get a small group of five to ten people from your customer base and encourage a discussion about your products or services using a set of questions. Qualitative methods can also include interviews and projective techniques like role-playing.

Once you have collected all this data, create a list of traits that you discovered in your research. Now narrow this list down to 10 or 12 that you would consider really important. This step can be a lot harder than you realise and sometimes you need to reconsider or even do further research if your marketing efforts are not working. The reason is that you could have missed something vitally important or your audience has changed.

The biggest benefit of creating our target market profile is that you can write directly to them as if you were speaking to them face to face.

The biggest mistake people make is to guess who their target audience is. Please don't do this, it does take time and effort to research, however, it will pay off in the end for you - the results will be amazing!

## The Top 5 Methods of Online Market Research

When it comes to market research, the internet is a blessing. Never has there been so much information about consumers and how they think right at your fingertips. In the past, marketing companies and businesses had to rely solely on costlier, more time consuming methods like focus groups, surveys and other data-gathering methods. Online research offers some excellent shortcuts.

Whenever you start an online marketing campaign, the most basic step is to gather relevant keywords. Keywords are essential but they don't get you much hard data about your target audience other than what they're searching for online.

Following are the top 5 methods used to do market research online.

**Online Surveys -** Online surveys allow you to ask your market questions anonymously and much of the process can be automated. This is also a viable method of conducting quantitative market research and discovering general trends.

**Blog Questions -** You can ask questions on your blog and encourage them to leave their input. By ending your blog post with a question, allows your audience to engage. People love to share their opinions and will do so eagerly.

**Your Email List -** Your list of email subscribers is a built-in, pre-screened audience that's great for seeking feedback.

**Forums and Q&A Sites -** Forums and question-and-answer sites offer data on all kinds of topics. This is a great place to gather information and see what problems people are having.

**Social Networks -** Social networks are places where people openly share their likes and interests. This gives you a great insight into what people are looking for and what interests they have.

Even though you can discover lots of information online, don't abandon your offline market research.

## How to Use Online Surveys to Research Your Market

To get the data you need to know, you have to create a survey that asks the right questions. If you can conduct your online survey correctly, you will gain invaluable information about how your target market thinks and shops.

Following are some tips to help you:

**Stick to One Issue -** Each survey should be on only one topic. Don't tackle everything all at once. Do multiple surveys for different types of information rather than overwhelm people and have them not complete your survey.

**What to Ask -** Your questions shouldn't be open-ended, leading, or potentially offensive to your respondents. In other words, be polite and ask questions they MUST answer.

**Tools to Make It Easier -** There are a number of tools designed to make creating, conducting and analysing surveys easier. The most popular is one called 'Survey Monkey'.

It's good to offer an incentive or reward for taking the time to participate in your survey. A good example of this would be to give them something in return, like a complimentary membership on your website, a coupon, or a free entry into a contest.

## Offline Methods for Conducting Market Research

You can do a great deal of market research on the Internet, but it's no substitute for offline research techniques.

**In-Person Surveys -** In-person surveys are usually conducted one-on-one in shopping centres or other public places. An advantage of this method is that you can show people your products and they can physically try them out before giving you a response.

**Focus Groups -** A focus group is a small group of people who meet to informally discuss your products. This group can be anywhere from five to ten people. As the moderator, you can lead the discussion using scripted questions and topics that relates to your business.

**Observations –** Observe shoppers in their natural habitat and conduct follow-up interviews if permissible. Observation shows you their real behaviour.

**Live Events -** Live events allow your customers to interact directly with your brand and products. The idea here is to get the participants as engaged as possible.

The best practice is to use both online and offline methods to learn about your target market. They will both reveal different data to you about your target market.

With online market research, you can gather information quickly and cheaply, where offline research gives you more access to primary sources of information and yields more in-depth results. The idea is not to rely on only one of these methods if you want to minimise your risk and maximise your chances for success.

## Learn About Your Market Through Your Blog

You can find out all kinds of information about your target market through your blog. This is the perfect way to interact with your audience and build a relationship.

**Ask a Question -** As mentioned above, end your blog posts with a question and encourage your readers to give their two cents. These opinions they give you as comments will allow you to learn some valuable qualitative data.

**Always Answer Comments -** Reply to all comments, letting them know that you're there and you're responsive to them. Get a conversation going so that you build the relationship with them.

**Email for more Information -** When you want to know more about a commenter's opinion, email them personally. This can sometimes be a better approach because they are more inclined to share their opinions privately with you.

**Making your Blog a Nice Neighbourhood -** Make your blog a supportive place where people aren't afraid to comment or ask questions. The way to do this is to be personable. Be friendly and welcoming and your readers will be more likely to interact with you.

**Use Comments for Future Posts -** Turn your readers' comments into future blog posts. This has a double benefit of having a ready source of information for future blog posts as well as giving your audience what they want.

**Spy on your Competition -** Read your competition's blog as well. See what their readers have to say; this could be another source of ideas for future blog posts.

**Beyond your Blog -** The same basic techniques can be used to engage customers and learn more about them on other sites as well.

**How to use Email to Better Understand your Market**

Email is a cheap, easy and fast way to find out more about your target market.

- **Email Makes it Easy -** The biggest advantage of email is that it makes responding easy. Email surveys are extremely easy for both you and your respondents.
- **Opinion Surveys by Email -** Opinion surveys require a little more from your respondents but can yield more in-depth information. These surveys are where you ask for suggestions or ideas and people respond with their opinions. Since you are asking for more information, this is a great time to offer an incentive or reward for participating.
- **The Dreaded Delete Button -** Keep your respondents from deleting your emails by clearly stating what the emails are all about and what they can expect. It is really important to make sure the 'from' line tells the recipient who you are and the 'subject' line needs to explain exactly what your email is about. Tell people why you want their input and you're going to use it to improve your products or services. A good thing is to also let them know how long the survey will take them.
- **Spicing up your Surveys -** Add images or other media to your email surveys to make them more interesting and will encourage engagement.
- **Take Advantage of Software Programs -** Software programs automate everything for you. As mentioned above, Survey Monkey makes market research through email so much easier for the end user. They have the capability to automate everything for you, from designing the surveys to analysing your results. They actually offer both

customisable features and templates, where you can change the questions accordingly.

- **Share the Results -** Share the results with your respondents through email or your blog. Let people know when they can expect to see the results of your survey and don't forget to thank them!

Before conducting surveys by email, make sure your target market is online. Some consumers aren't. Yes, there are still people that don't have or use emails! Email surveys work best for groups that use it often like business people, students, association members, or subscribers to your list. This is important to remember when you are planning your survey.

## Fly on the Wall – Where to go Online to Listen to your Market

The internet offers lots of great places to go and listen to your target market give their opinions and share their interests. This is the absolute best way to find out what your market wants and needs.

If you listen and watch carefully, you will see a pattern emerge of a problem your target audience is having. Once you know what that is, you need to act immediately and offer them the solution to their problem!

- **Forums and Q and A Sites -** Forums and question-and-answer sites show you what topics are hot and what people are saying about them.

Look at the members who are most active and leave the most replies. This tells you that they love sharing their opinion and they'll happily do so for you.

You can discover other priceless insights by looking at what people are saying. Read threads that are relevant to your products or services and they'll tell you exactly what people are looking for. You can search these sites for keywords and if you don't find what you need, start your own thread asking for opinions.

- **Social Networking Sites -** Social networking sites allow you to interact directly with your target market and discover exactly what they're into.
  No matter where you go to listen to your market, the flow is the same:

Identify your market, find out where they hang out, and use that site to gather information about them.

One of the reasons social media sites are great for market research is that they have detailed profiles. By looking at your customers' profiles, you can find out what other interests they have. This is a great source of non-demographic information, like how they see themselves, what they think about current events, or how they use the products they buy.

One key difference with social media is that you need to be more subtle. When you ask a pointed marketing question, it may put people off. Social media sites are used for entertainment and socialising mostly. People like to hang out online with their friends and share content they like. Take a friendly and personal approach. It helps if you have a lot of friends already on the site that you interact with casually.

Facebook is still the largest social media network, but it's good to have a presence on as many networks as possible. Each offers unique ways to do market research. For example, on YouTube you can see which videos are getting the most views.

## Your Perfect Customer – How to Create a Target Market Profile

The goal of market research is to create a profile of your perfect customer. The point of market research is to gather data and give you a comprehensive picture of your target market. When businesses do this, they create a unique customer profile. This is the ideal customer who wants and needs your products, and it's very detailed.

A good customer profile must be as specific as possible. Lots of companies go so far as to give them names and draw images. They may even have pictures of real people who represent their market.

- **Demographic Information -** Demographic information is data about your customer including age, gender, location, education level, income and family structure.
- Example: your customer might be a 30-year-old mum that is a working professional that lives in the suburbs of a large city. Or perhaps it is a male who earns over $100,000 per year.
- **Lifestyle and Hobbies -** What your customers do on the weekends and their interests are also important. Some examples of lifestyle and hobby data include:
- Free time activities
- Eating and health habits
- Smoking and drinking
- Clubs and organisations they belong to
- Places they frequent

All of these are equally important. For example, you might be targeting a well-to-do male in their twenties who enjoys the nightlife on the weekends. If your product or service is related to the outdoors, your ideal customer is active on weekends camping, snowboarding, camping, and doing other outdoor activities.

- **Morals and Values -** Learn how they see themselves and how they feel about the world around them. You will also want to clearly define their attitude and beliefs about themselves, about current events, and products like yours. You would also want to know what their goals and aspirations are, and where they see themselves in the future.

- **Pain Points -** Pain points are essential because you're going to be offering your book as a solution. You need to define what frustrates them, what they worry about or fear, and what problems they currently face. It's also a good thing to know what kinds of solutions they are looking for.
- **Shopping Habits -** How they shop and use the products they buy is also key information. Your profile should address how people in your market shop. This includes how much they spend, where they like to shop (online vs. offline) and how they use the products they buy. It's your job to connect them to the right products where and when they are looking for them.

Note: You need as specific a picture as possible or you run the risk of casting your net too wide.

## Keeping Track of your Changing Market

People's tastes change and you need to keep researching your market. If your message doesn't keep up with the times, it can become irrelevant very quickly. A product that was perfectly matched to your target market one month ago can and will become passé the next.

- **Conduct Regular Market Research -** Make market research a regular part of your business's operations. It is not a one-shot deal. You must keep doing this on a consistent basis. Whatever methods you use to conduct research, work them into your regular schedule. Don't just conduct a research when you a have a new book to launch or a problem with your sales.
- **Improve your Offerings -** Use the data you gather to improve your products and services. People that stay in touch with their audience and seek feedback discover better ways to help them solve their problems. You will improve your knowledge of your market's tastes, likes, needs and wants every time you do more research.
- **Keep in Touch Online -** Stay in communication with your market through the internet. You really need to keep the channels of communication open at all times. Here are some great ways to do that:
- **Social Media.** Maintain a strong social media presence and interact daily with your fans and followers.
- **Blogging.** Regularly write a company blog and try to get interaction and conversation going among readers.
- **Online Surveys.** Conduct surveys and analyse results on a regular basis.
- **Feedback Forms.** Everywhere possible, give your customers a feedback form where they can leave an anonymous comment about your services.
- **Online Forums.** Keep abreast of what's going on

among your customers and in your industry by spending time on forums related to your business.

- **Sign up for Alerts -** Sign up for alert services so that you'll know whenever your name or business's name is mentioned. One free program that does this is Google Alerts. Whenever your name or business's name appears anywhere online, you'll get an email telling you. The email will contain a link so that you can go directly to the website where you've been mentioned.
- Whenever someone says anything about you, whether good or bad, you'll know it. This is very valuable feedback; a bad listing tells you what you need to improve. Alerts also give you the heads-up when you need to do some damage control from a negative mention.

**Don't make Assumptions -** When businesses fail to conduct ongoing market research, they make one of the deadliest assumptions possible. They assume that their market's tastes won't change over time and their products will always continue to be in demand. On the other hand, companies that keep their ears open stay in the loop and can change with the times. When it comes to marketing, never assume and never just "hope" you'll get it right. Base your marketing decisions on hard data collected directly from your target market.

Knowing your target audience is crucial. Why not join us for an interactive workshop to find out who your ideal customer is?

# Chapter Six

## Knowing Your Audience Completely

*"Success is knowing exactly who your audience is"*

It is really important that you understand your audience, especially if you want to be successful each and every time you communicate with them. In this chapter we will take a look at another two methods where we are going to uncover how you can identify the different behaviours and personality types of your audience.

If you think about the interactions you currently have in your day, you will no doubt have had one of those days where you have a very successful interaction with one person and in the next minute you completely have no connection at all to that person. There is a good reason why this happens and this chapter will uncover how you can be successful with every person you come into contact with, especially when they are reading your book.

So let's take a closer look:

What influences your behaviour?

What influences the behaviour of others?

## What influences behaviour?

When we observe others we are observing their behaviour.

What we see is just the tip of the iceberg; their behaviour is the outcome of an extremely complex mix of psychological factors.

- Why do people behave the way they do?
- What causes one reaction in one person and a completely different reaction in another?
- What influences a person's behaviour?

## Predictability

Human behaviour is, to a large degree, predictable. Once you get to really know a person you can, with a certain degree of accuracy, determine how they will behave under normal circumstances.

There are broad bands of behaviour that are predictable due to cultural, educational and social conditioning. This is why it is important to find out exactly who your audience is.

By observing a person's past behaviour and understanding the patterns they usually follow, you can quite accurately predict how they will behave in a similar situation in the future, this will especially help you when you are writing your book, knowing how they will react is critical.

## Perception

Perception is what our *mind* sees, not what our eye sees. Reality deals with logic and fact, perception deals with a mix of logic, fact, emotions, feelings, experience, personal interpretation and prejudice.

We filter our observations of the behaviour of others through a series of complex personal filters.

# Behavioural Styles Questionnaire

## Please read these instructions carefully

1.  Relax and be objective about yourself – there are no right or wrong answers

2.  Answer the questions as you know you are, not as you would like to be

3.  Determine which of the four comments MOST accurately describes you and place a number 4 on that line

4.  Decide which of the remaining three comments NEXT MOST is like you then place a number 3 on that line

5.  Rank the remaining two comments by placing a number 2 and then 1 on the appropriate line, so that number 1 is LEAST like you of all four comments

6.  Answer all sections in a like manner

7.  Check your answers when complete to be sure that all statements have the four comments rated from 1 to 4 using each number only once

| Remember: | 4 is MOST like you |
| --- | --- |
| | 1 is LEAST like you |

**When I am at work I am:**

- ☐ Correct and accurate
- ☐ Outgoing and enthusiastic
- ☐ Dependable and reliable
- ☐ Efficient and quick to get on with the job

**I work best with people who are:**

- ☐ Self controlled, able to sort out the facts to get the job done.
- ☐ Fun to be with and are motivating
- ☐ Supportive of other people, considerate of personal objectives
- ☐ Independent, able to get on with their work with minimum supervision

## I feel of most value when I can:

- ☐ Work out the details of a new concept or idea at my own pace
- ☐ Motivated others towards goals that I consider important
- ☐ Show others how to practically apply a new idea or concept
- ☐ Get others to expand themselves

## When people upset me I feel like:

- ☐ Avoiding them and getting on with other things that are important to me
- ☐ Telling them how I feel about the situation in no uncertain manner
- ☐ Agreeing with them to avoid the personal conflict
- ☐ Confronting them and telling them what is wrong

## I lead people by:

- ☐ Consulting with them to ensure that they stay on track
- ☐ Creating open, active discussions to build personal motivation
- ☐ Sharing how I feel about the situation to gain their support
- ☐ Directing them toward the achievement of the job at hand

## I am a person who:

- ☐ Is disciplined and thorough at everything I do
- ☐ Enjoys social interaction and companionship
- ☐ Understand other people well enough not to cause personal conflicts
- ☐ Is tough and demanding, but always fair

## When I have an important decision to make, I consider:

- ☐ The facts that I personally have found to be correct

- ☐ Recommendations made by people I respect

- ☐ The opinions and feelings of the people closest to me

- ☐ The various options available, to arrive at the best alternative

## When I am asked to help another person, I:

- ☐ Take my time to observe the situation, and then discuss what can be done

- ☐ Confront them as quickly as possible to help them get back on track

- ☐ Be supportive of their situation, so that I can understand how they feel

- ☐ Discover what their problem is and then tell them what they need to do

**Close friends would most likely describe me as:**

- ☐ Reliable, dependable and well organised
- ☐ A fun loving person who has a good personality
- ☐ Trustworthy and a good friend to have when in need
- ☐ Opinionated and headstrong, but often right!

**When I am under emotional stress:**

- ☐ Withdraw to avoid the people causing me the stress
- ☐ Sometimes do hurtful things that I later regret
- ☐ I become personally hurt by the thoughtless actions of other people
- ☐ I am easy to anger

**When I meet people for the first time, I am:**

- ☐ Careful to project a favourable appearance
- ☐ Sociable and friendly to relax them and get to know them quickly
- ☐ Friendly, but take time to establish a relationship
- ☐ Myself, whether they like me or not

## When working with other people, I am:

- ☐ Accurate and well organised
- ☐ Creative and involved in a variety of activities
- ☐ Friendly and part of the team
- ☐ In charge (and/or) actively involved in getting the job done

## When socialising, I usually:

- ☐ Have a quiet formal dinner party with close acquaintances
- ☐ Enjoy a fast paced party with a variety of people
- ☐ Have a relaxed, informal, casual get together
- ☐ Be private, sharing best with only one other

## When in close relationship with another person, I:

- ☐ Am discreet and proper, not openly demonstrating my feelings to others

- ☐ Show my affection openly, enjoying close contact

- ☐ Enjoy a close, gentle association demonstrating warmth

- ☐ Take it or leave it, as I consider it is not necessary to continually give or receive affection to prove it exists.

## When communicating with other people, I:

- ☐ Take my time, asking them what they think about the matter

- ☐ Am open, prepared to negotiate to achieve my objectives

- ☐ Am tactful and sensitive to their feelings about the situation

- ☐ Get to the point and tell them how I see the situation

Now that you have completed the project, please total the numbers as follows:

**Total of first squares** _____

**Total of second squares** _____

**Total of third squares** _____

**Total of fourth squares** _____

**Total** 150

Now plot your first square number onto (1)

in the picture following.

Same, plot your second square number onto (2)

Plot your third square total onto (3)

Finally, plot your fourth square total along (4)

Now join the four dots into a kite or box type.

Task Focused, Formal
Cool, Independent, Uncommunicative,
Guarded, Disciplined about time

**Conscientious (1)**

**Dominance (4)**

56

56

42

42

28

28

15

15

Introverted
Passive
Co-operative
Slow actions
Avoids risks

Extroverted
Assertive
Competitive
Fast actions
Takes risks

15

15

28

28

42

42

56

56

**Steadiness (3)**

**Influence (2)**

Social Aspects, Casual
Warm, Approachable, Communicative,
Open, Undisciplined about time,
Uses opinions

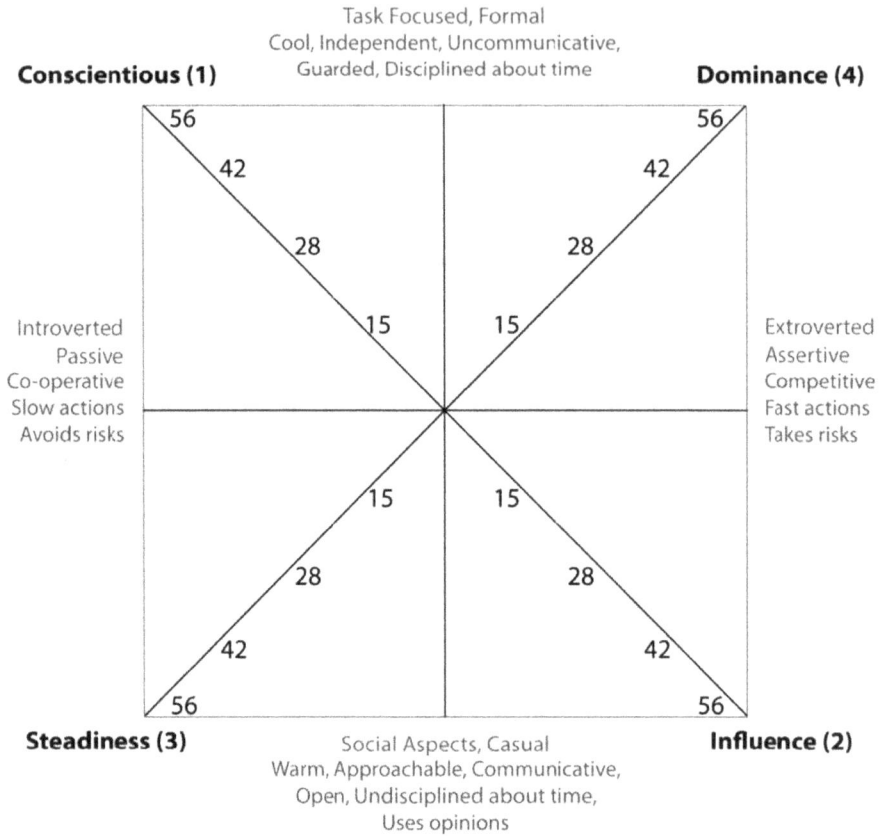

DISC provides a common language that you can use to better understand not only yourself but also to be able to adapt your behaviour to others. Understanding this will help you write your book to the different types of behaviours in people.

**D**ominance - relating to control, power and assertiveness

**I**nfluence - relating to social situations and communication

**S**teadiness - relating to patience, persistence, and thoughtfulness

**C**onscientiousness - relating to structure and organisation

These four dimensions can be grouped in a grid with D and I sharing the top row and representing extroverted aspects of the personality, and C and S below representing introverted aspects. D and C then share the left column and represent task-focused aspects, and I and S share the right column and represent social aspects. In this matrix, the vertical dimension represents a factor of **"Assertive"** or **"Passive"**, while the horizontal represents **"Open"** vs. **"Guarded"**.

**Dominance**: People who score high in the intensity of the 'D' styles factor are very active in dealing with problems and challenges, while low D scores are people who want to do more research before committing to a decision. High "D" people are described as demanding, forceful, egocentric, strong willed, driving, determined, ambitious, aggressive, and pioneering. Low D scores describe those who are conservative, low-keyed, cooperative, calculating, undemanding, cautious, mild, agreeable, modest and peaceful.

**Influence**: People with High I scores influence others through talking and activity and tend to be emotional. They are described as convincing, magnetic, political, enthusiastic, persuasive, warm, demonstrative, trusting, and optimistic. Those with Low I scores influence more by data and facts, and not with feelings. They are described as reflective, factual, calculating, skeptical, logical, suspicious, matter of fact, pessimistic, and critical.

**Steadiness**: People with High S styles scores want a steady pace, security, and do not like sudden change. Low S intensity scores are those who like change and variety. High S persons are calm, relaxed, patient, possessive, predictable, deliberate, stable, consistent, and tend to be unemotional and poker faced. People with Low S scores are described as restless, demonstrative, impatient, eager, or even impulsive.

**Conscientiousness**: Persons with High C styles adhere to rules, regulations, and structure. They like to do quality work and do it right the first time. High C people are careful, cautious, exacting, neat, systematic, diplomatic, accurate, and tactful. Those with Low C scores challenge the rules and want independence and are described as self-willed, stubborn, opinionated, unsystematic, arbitrary, and careless with details.

## How do you and others learn best?

The following questionnaire aims to find out something about your preferences for the way you work with information. You will have a preferred learning style and one part of that learning style is your preference for the intake and output of ideas and information.

Choose the answer which best explains your preference and tick the box next to the letter. Please select more than one response if a single answer does not match your perception. Leave blank any question, which does not apply.

1. You are about to give directions to a person who is standing with you. She is staying in a hotel in town and wants to visit your house later. She has a rental car.
   Would you?

☐    a. draw a map on paper.

☐    b. tell her the directions

☐    c. write down the directions (without a map)

☐    d. collect her from the hotel in your car.

2. You are not sure whether a word should be spelled 'dependent' or 'dependant'. Do you:?

☐    c. look it up in the dictionary.

☐    a.  see the word in your mind and choose by the way it looks

☐    b. sound it out in your mind.

☐    d. write both versions down on paper and choose one.

3. You have just received a copy of your itinerary for a world trip. This is of interest to a friend. Would you?

☐    b. phone her immediately and tell her about it.

☐    c. send her a copy of the printed itinerary

☐    a. show her on a map of the world.

☐    d. share what you plan to do at each place you visit.

4. You are going to cook something as a special treat for your family. Do you?

- ☐ d. cook something familiar without the need for instructions.

- ☐ a. thumb through the cookbook looking for ideas from the pictures.

- ☐ c. refer to a specific cookbook where there is a good recipe.

5. A group of tourists have been assigned to you to find out about wildlife reserves or parks. Would you?

- ☐ d. drive them to a wildlife reserve or park.

- ☐ a. show them slides and photographs.

- ☐ c. give them pamphlets or a book on wildlife reserves or parks.

- ☐ b. give them a talk on wildlife reserves or parks.

6. You are about to purchase a new stereo. Other than price, what would most influence your decision?

☐ b. the salesperson telling you what you want to know.

☐ c. reading the details about it.

☐ d. playing with the controls and listening to it.

☐ a. it looks really smart and fashionable.

7. Recall a time in your life when you learned how to do something like playing a new board game. Try to avoid choosing a very physical skill, e.g. riding a bike. How did you learn best? By:

☐ a. visual clues -- pictures, diagrams, charts.

☐ c. written instructions.

☐ b. listening to somebody explaining it.

☐ d. doing it or trying it.

8.  You have an eye problem. Would you prefer that the doctor?

☐   b. tell you what is wrong.

☐   a. show you a diagram of what is wrong.

☐   d. use a model to show you what is wrong.

9.  You are about to learn to use a new program on a computer. Would you?

☐   d. sit down at the keyboard and begin to experiment with the program's features.

☐   c. read the manual which comes with the program.

☐   b. telephone a friend and ask questions about it.

10. You are staying in a hotel and have a rental car. You would like to visit friends whose address/location you do not know. Would you like them to?

☐    a. draw you a map on paper.

☐    b. tell you the directions.

☐    c. write down the directions (without a map).

☐    d. collect you from the hotel in their car.

11. Apart from the price, what would most influence your decision to buy a particular textbook?

☐    d. you have used a copy before.

☐    b. a friend talking about it.

☐    c. quickly reading parts of it.

☐    a. the way it looks is appealing.

12. A new movie has arrived in town. What would most influence your decision to go (or not go)?

☐ b. you heard a radio review about it.

☐ c. you read a review about it.

☐ a. you saw a preview of it.

13. Do you prefer a lecturer or teacher who likes to use?

☐ c. a textbook, handouts, readings

☐ a. flow diagrams, charts, slides.

☐ d. field trips, labs, practical sessions.

☐ b. discussion, guest speakers.

When you have finished making your selections count up how many answers you have marked in total, and then how many A's, B's, C's and D's. The following table shows you what type of learning style is best for you. So if you have more A's than the other letters, then your learning style is 'Visual'.

| A | B | C | D |
|---|---|---|---|
| | | | |
| Visual | Auditory | Read/Write (Auditory Digital) | Kinesthetic |

VARK is the understanding of learning styles that shows you how individuals have a preferential way in which they absorb, process, comprehend and retain information. In other words, some people prefer verbal instructions, while others prefer visuals or hands-on interaction. Knowing this kind of information is very important when you are writing your book, you need to know how to deliver your information via your book.

VARK is a short, simple inventory whose dimensions are intuitively understood and whose applications are practical. Its use has helped people to learn more effectively and mentors to become more sensitive to the diversity of teaching strategies necessary to reach all learners.

## A Brief Overview of VARK

VARK is an acronym made from the initial letters of

four sensory preferences (Visual, Auditory, Read/write (Auditory Digital) and Kinesthetic). Preferences are used by people when they are taking in or giving out information. For example some people prefer to 'read about it,' others to talk or draw. Some have no strong preferences for any one mode.

**Visual (V):**

This preference includes the depiction of information in charts, graphs, flow charts, and all the symbolic arrows, circles, hierarchies and other devices that instructors use to represent what could have been presented in words. They love colour.

**Auditory (A):**

This perceptual mode describes a preference for information that is "heard." People with this modality report that they learn best from lectures, tutorials, tapes, and talking to other people.

**Read/Write (Auditory Digital) (R):**

This preference is for information displayed as words. Not surprisingly, many academics, accountants, lawyers, engineers have a strong preference for this modality.

## Kinesthetic (K):

By definition, this modality refers to the perceptual preference related to the use of experience and practice (simulated or real). Although such an experience may invoke other modalities, the key is that the student is connected to reality, either through experience, example, practice or simulation.

## Visual Strategies

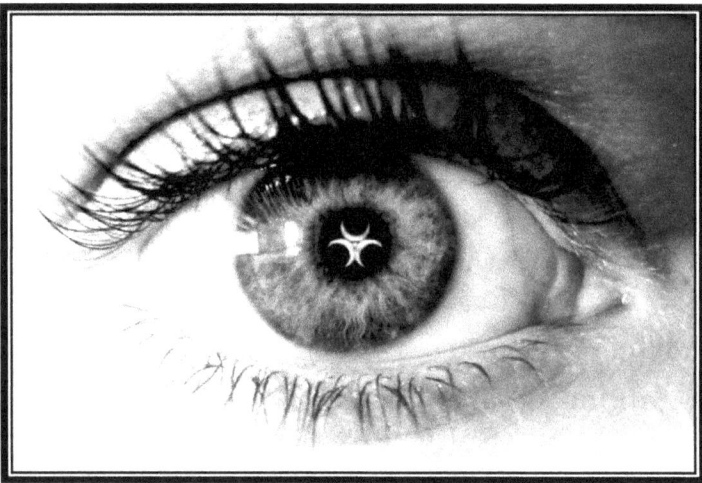

For those with a strong preference for Visual learning, you should use some or all of the following:

To help them take in the information, use:

- Underlining
- Different colours
- Highlighters
- Symbols
- Flowcharts
- Charts
- Graphs
- Pictures
- Different spatial arrangements on the page
- White space

These people are holistic rather than reductionist in their approach. They want the whole picture. Visual learners do not like handouts, words, lectures, textbooks or assessment that hinge on word usage, syntax and grammar. They are going to watch TV!

**Visual Words**

| | | |
|---|---|---|
| See | Bright | View |
| Show | Clear | Illustrate |
| Picture | Perceive | Focused |

| | | |
|---|---|---|
| Look | Highlight | Perspective |
| Envision | Reflect | Preview |
| Watch | Appear | Dawn |
| Reveal | Illuminate | Imagine |
| Crystal | | |

## Examples at work

- Let me have a **look** at it for you
- I will **see** if I can do anything
- **Show** me the specific numbers and we will **see** what we can do
- Let me run the numbers and that will give me a **clear** picture

## Auditory Strategies

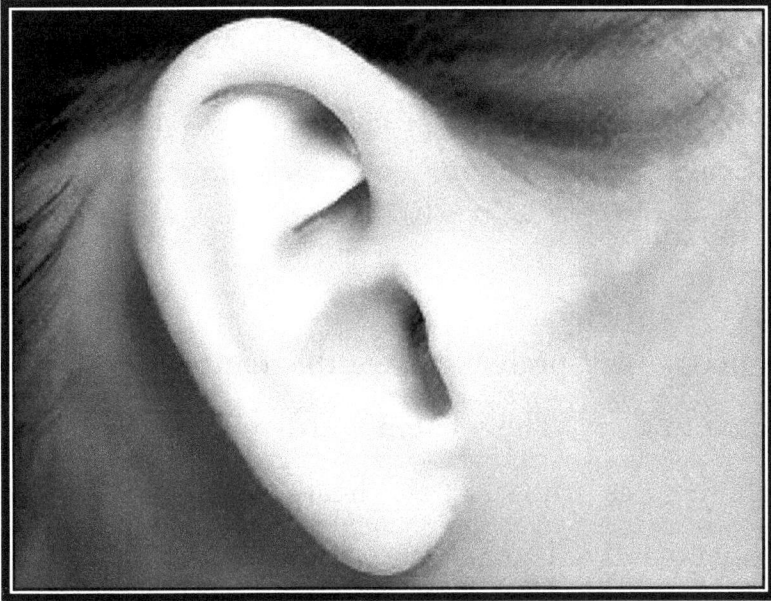

For those with a strong preference for learning by Auditory methods you should use some or all of the following:

To help them take in the information use:

- Links to Lectures and tutorials
- Links to discussion of topics with other people
- Get them to discuss and explain the ideas in your book with other people

- Interesting examples, stories, jokes
- Describe the pictures and other visuals you have in your book
- Leave spaces in your book for later recall and 'filing'

These people will prefer to have this entire page explained to them. The written words will not be as valuable as those they hear. They will probably go and tell somebody about this!

## Auditory Words

| Say | Tell | Tone |
| --- | --- | --- |
| Static | Rings a bell | Sound |
| Speak | Express | Mention |
| Accent | Resonate | Remark |
| Ask | Unique | Hear |

Talk                Listen              Make music

Tune in/out         Silence             Be all ears

Be heard            Question            Unhearing

## Examples at Work

- I will **speak** with the publisher about your book and they will **tell** us if we can make it work

- **Sounds** good, send me the details and I will **ask** if we can make those words work

- I will **talk** to our team, **express** your concerns and let's wait to **hear** what they say

## Read/Write (Auditory Digital) Strategies

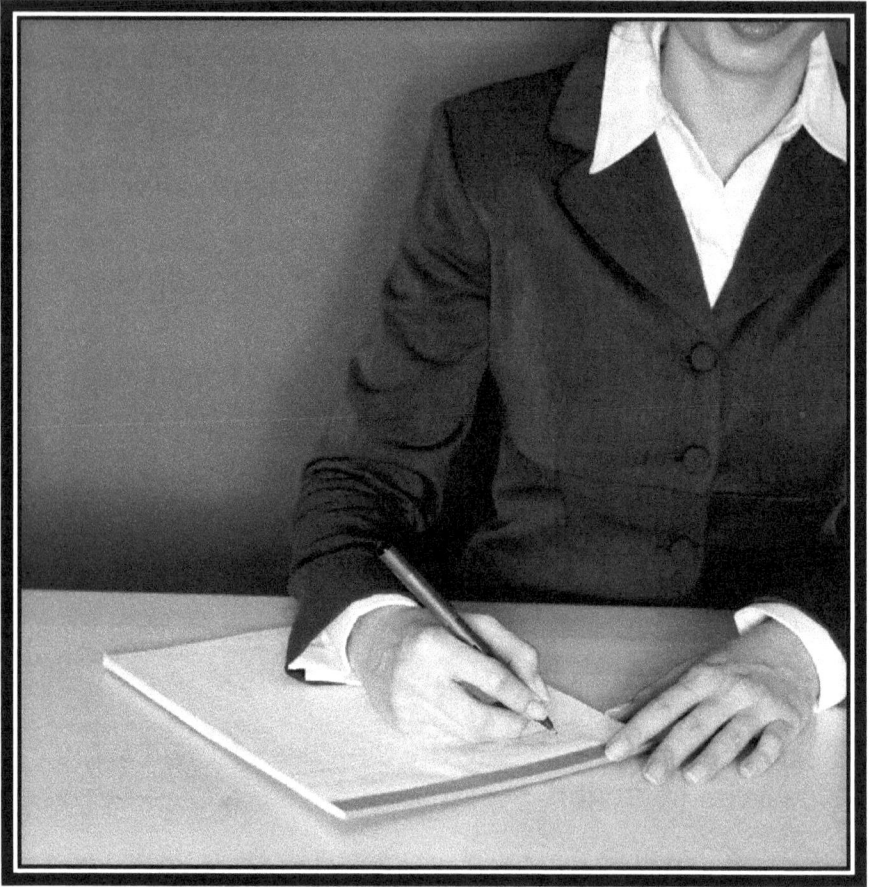

For those who have a strong preference for learning by reading/writing you should use some or all of the following:

To help them take in the information, use:

- Lists
- Headings
- Dictionaries
- Glossaries
- Definitions
- Links to Handouts
- Links to Textbooks
- Links to Readings - Library
- Links to Manuals (computing and laboratory)

These people will like this page because the emphasis is on words and lists. They believe that the meanings are within the words, so reading your book was OK, but a link to a handout is better. They will shortly be heading for the library to do further research.

## Kinesthetic Strategies

For those who have a strong preference for Kinesthetic learning you should use some or all of the following:

To help them take in the information, use:

- All your senses - sight, touch, taste, smell, hearing (this an be challenging when writing your book, this is where your talent will shine when you can explain the different senses in your book through your words!
- Examples of principles
- Links to mentors who give real-life examples
- Applications
- Hands-on approaches
- Samples and photographs

These people want to experience the results so that they can understand it. The ideas on this page are only valuable if they sound practical, real and relevant. They need to do things to understand.

## Kinesthetic Words

| | | |
|---|---|---|
| Feel | Grab | Touch |
| Get a handle | Rub | Grasp |
| Affect | Impress | Hit |
| Suffer | Tackle | Pressure |
| Know | Intuition | Make contact |
| Get hold of | Slip through | Catch on |
| Tap into | Throw out | Turn around |
| Hard | Unfeeling | Concrete |

## Examples at Work

- Let me **get a handle** on your proposal

- Once I have **grasped** the numbers, we can **tackle** the situation better

- I need to **know** specifics, send it to me and I will be able to get a **feel** for the numbers and how we can **affect** things our end for you

# Part Two - Let's Demystify How To Create Your Book

# Chapter Seven

# Finding Peace, Passion & Purpose

*"The creation of your first book will be the proudest moment of your life"*

It's now time to create your chapters! The way we do this is by unpacking the titles of each chapter. By that I mean we drill down and work out the words that best describe each chapter and what the sub topics will be.

Get yourself a pen and notepad. I want you to turn off all your distractions, like your phone, email etc. Set a timer for one hour. Next, follow the steps below and do not stop until the time goes off:

NOTE: It is a good idea to photocopy the worksheet so you can re-order your list easily.

- List 12 to 16 topics in the following outline worksheet
- Now put that list into order
- Next, list 4 sub topics for each of those original topics
- Now put your sub topics into order

## Outline Worksheet

**1. Identify your main topic**
**2. Identify your main categories (these will be your chapters)**
**3. Identify your sub-topics (should have a minimum of 2-4 per chapter)**

# MAIN TOPIC

_____

_____

# Category

_____

# Sub-topics (and if necessary, sub-subcategories)

_____

_____

_____

_____

# Category

_____

# Sub-topics (and if necessary, sub-subcategories)

_____

_____

_____

_____

# Category

_____

# Sub-topics (and if necessary, sub-subcategories)

_____

_____

_____

_____

# Category

_____

# Sub-topics (and if necessary, sub-subcategories)

_____

_____

_____

_____

# Category

_____

# Sub-topics (and if necessary, sub-topics)

_____

_____

_____

_____

# Category

_____

# Sub-topics (and if necessary, sub-topics)

_____

_____

_____

_____

## Category

_____

## Sub-topics (and if necessary, sub-sub-topics)

_____

_____

_____

_____

## Category

_____

## Sub-topics (and if necessary, sub-sub-topics)

_____

_____

_____

_____

## Category

_____

## Sub-topics (and if necessary, sub-sub-topics)

_____

_____

_____

_____

## Category

_____

## Sub-topics (and if necessary, sub-sub-topics)

_____

_____

_____

_____

## Category

_____

## Sub-topics (and if necessary, sub-sub-topics)

_____

_____

_____

_____

## Category

_____

## Sub-topics (and if necessary, sub-sub-topics)

_____

_____

_____

_____

## Category

_____

## Sub-topics (and if necessary, sub-topics)

_____

_____

_____

_____

## Category

_____

## Sub-topics (and if necessary, sub-topics)

_____

_____

_____

_____

## Category

_____

## Sub-topics (and if necessary, sub-sub-topics)

_____

_____

_____

_____

## Category

_____

## Sub-topics (and if necessary, sub-sub-topics)

_____

_____

_____

_____

When the timer is finished, take a break, get yourself a glass of water or a cup of coffee/tea. Sit back and take a look at what you have just created. This is the outline of your book! The next step is to tidy up the topics, which are the chapters of your book.

You need to make each chapter have a sexy heading, to do this I have included how I created mine for this book:

**PART ONE – The Psychology behind writing**

Chapter 1. Introduction          *"How it all Started"*

Chapter 2. Everyone has a book in them *"The Author Within"*

- What is your burning desire for writing a book? *"Your Burning Desire"*

- Why doesn't everyone write a book? (Writer's block) *"Only the Special Accomplish Great Success"*

Chapter 3. Focus and concentration    *"Setting the Stage"*

- The art of storytelling    *"Stories that sell"*

Chapter 4. The psychology behind writing your book *"Expressing your Thoughts"*

Chapter 5. Target market     *"Who is your audience?"*

Chapter 6. DISC & VARK     *"Knowing your Audience Completely"*

**PART TWO – Let's Demystify Creating Your Book!**

Chapter 7. Create chapters - Unpack titles & topics

*"Finding Peace, Passion & Purpose"*

- Writing tools          *"Tools of the Trade"*

- Mind mapping           *"Start from the Centre"*

Chapter 8.  What to write about? *"Ready, Set, GO!"*

- Killer Headlines & emotional triggers
  *"Getting Noticed"*

Chapter 9.  Write your book *"Don't Judge a Book by its Cover"*

- Where to look for inspiration & ideas  *"What's in a Name?"*

- Create your book cover  *"Sell to the World"*

- Images & Quotes   *"Daily Strengths for Daily needs"*

- TOC, Disclaimer, Copyright, EIN, ISBN
  *"Tying up Loose ends"*

Chapter 10.  Proofreading & Editing *"Eliminate Embarrassing Writing Errors"*

- Createspace          *"Your Publishing Friend"*

- Upload book          *"Lift off!!"*

Chapter 11.  Publish & Profit *"Connecting the dots"*

- Promote yourself         *"Promote your Expertise Through Various Channels"*

## Tools of the Trade

Before you start writing your book, it is highly recommended that you use the method of a "Mind Map" to layout your book ideas. On the following pages, I show you how to use mind maps to write your book. Once you have your mind map complete then you can begin to write, following are a couple of tools that you can use:

The free option for writing your book is to use Microsoft "Word". Once completed you will need to export it as a PDF to be ready for publishing. See chapter 10, section 4 called "Lift Off!" for instructions to download a "Word" template that is available on

Createspace.

Scrivener is a great tool for writers. It is a wonderful tool that allows you to keep all your information in one place for easy access. It helps you format your book quickly and easily and it helps you to export your book when you are finished and ready to get published!

Look at the resources chapter for the link to where you can purchase Scrivener.

## Start from the Centre

### Mind Mapping as a Tool for creating your book

Mind mapping is a powerful tool for accomplishing a wide variety of things. It's a much better way to organise your thoughts than simply jotting down a list on paper. Your brain doesn't work in a linear way, so why organise in a linear way?

This is the idea behind mind mapping. Mind maps visually represent information, ideas, and structures in a way that immediately shows relationships. In effect, they're better suited to the human brain.

Once you know how to create useful, effective mind maps for your book, you'll find yourself with renewed creativity and a capacity to handle the challenges you face with more confidence.

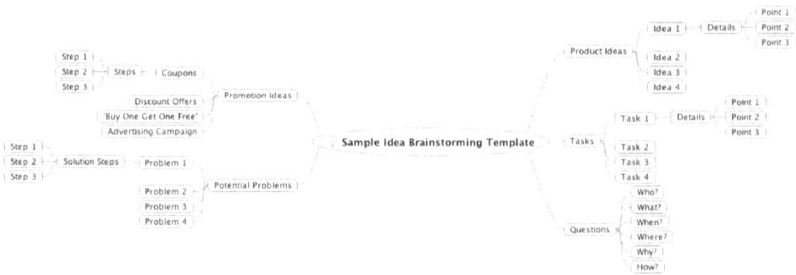

Sample Idea Brainstorming Template

Mind maps essentially work from the centre out. Your main idea is at the centre and the sub-topics go out like branches. This organisation allows you to take in the big picture at a glance. You can see which elements are the biggest or most important by how close they are to the centre.

## Emphasis on Relationships

Even a very simple mind map can convey complex relationships to those who look at it. You can see how the elements are linked together without having to have it all explained to you. This speeds up the understanding of a complex system.

## Mind Maps Are Fluid

It's easy to add new information to a mind map. With a list, your only choice is to add the new information at the bottom. Mind maps allow much greater flexibility and this comes in handy when there are small changes to your complex system.

## Visual Format

One of the reasons the human brain loves mind maps is that they're visual. This makes the information in them easier to understand and recall. With a list, outline, or detailed text, you have to slog through it to find specific key points or identify relationships. With a mind map, you can not only read, but actually 'see' the system as a whole.

## Anything Goes

Finally, you can use mind maps for anything. This is a simple and easy-to-master tool that can be applied to any situation in any area of your life. You can use mind maps to organise business projects, lay out complex structures, plan your product development, manage and track progress on business goals, brainstorm creative ideas, and more. They can also be used for projects, goals, and ideas in other areas of your life as well. However, we are going to concentrate on your book.

To get started mind mapping, you really only need a pen and paper. However, there are many other tools that can help you make better mind maps. Please see the resources chapter for more information.

## Mind Mapping with Pen and Paper

Even if you plan to use tools for making your maps, it's good to try making one on paper first. Take a piece of paper no larger than a letter or A4 sheet. Start by writing down the central idea or problem in the middle. Draw each related idea as a branch that comes out from the centre. Take a look at the image of the mind map shown on page 150 as an example. Write the idea and circle it, and then draw a line connecting it to the main idea. Take each of your related ideas and then jot down ideas related to them in the same way. Keep working outward like this until you feel you've written everything down, at least for now.

## Mind Mapping with Post-Its

Another way to make mind maps using simple tools is to use Post-It notes or stickers. The advantage of this method is that you can move the stickers around easily. Instead of writing down each idea and circling it, write each idea down on a Post-It and stick it where appropriate. You can create a mind map on a wall or whiteboard using this technique as well.

## Mind Mapping with a Whiteboard

If you want to try making a mind map with a group of people, use a whiteboard. This is a good method because it's easy to erase and move things. Put the topic in the middle of the board and then branch out from there.

## Mind Mapping Software and Apps

There are several software programs and apps that you can use for mind mapping. Once you've done a little mapping with your pen and paper, you'll have the experience to judge which program is best for you. There are plenty of free programs and premium programs with free trials as well. Please see the resources chapter for more information.

## Best Practices for Mind Mapping

When creating your mind map, free associate and write down ideas as quickly as they come to you. Don't try to explain each idea. Simply jot down a word or short phrase that indicates the idea. A mind map shouldn't be cluttered with text. Remember that it all needs to be taken in at a glance. You can expand your maps to include more details. Then once you complete the first steps, you can bring in the bigger picture.

In addition to words and phrases, you can draw images that remind you of concepts. The point is to communicate the main idea, not the details.

Keep branching out until you run out of ideas. You may

find yourself adding something later on. This is one of the things that make mind maps so useful. You may find it best to create rough draft mind maps on paper and then create more complete digital versions after. This way, you have a chance to map everything out once and see where it goes before you create the official map.

## Tips for Managing and Organising Information with Mind Maps

As a general rule, as I have already mentioned, a mind map should have as little text as possible, and this is definitely true when you're organising information. Don't go into detail, if there is more information that needs to be added, either create a new branch for this information or put a link to it.

Colour coding, symbols, and graphics are especially useful for organising information. They're more visually appealing and also communicate relationships in a more immediate way. When note taking, they also speed up the process of getting everything down.

A good technique for informational mind maps is to create floating topics for things that are difficult to place on the map. Place these ideas in the top corner of your paper mind map for later reference. If you have a new piece of information and you're not sure where it goes, set it aside and connect it later. Don't spend time trying to figure out where it goes.

## Tips for Planning with Mind Maps

Something like a book strategy is such a huge topic that it's usually a good idea to create one general mind map and then create other mind maps to cover main points (your characters, the story line, and your chapters). For example, each branch on your general mind map is a chapter in your book. Make a general map and then go back and create a more detailed map for each of these chapters that will then include your sub-topics.

When planning a project, make sure that each branch ends with an action plan and a deadline for getting that action plan done. You can then easily understand exactly what needs to be done as you move through the project by looking at the map.

After making a project mind map, go back and see if it's complete. There is often something you've forgotten that needs to be added later. Also, keep in mind that the project will change as you move through it.

## Mind Mapping Common Mistakes

Here are the common mistakes first-time mind mappers often make.

## Too Much Text

The beauty of a mind map is that it conveys a great deal of information at a glance. You don't have to include every single detail, just words, phrases, and main ideas. If you include too much text, you're no longer able to take the map in quickly. If you want to include more details, provide links to more information. Keep your mind maps simple and uncluttered.

## Massive Mind Maps

It may seem natural that a bigger mind map means you can stuff more ideas into it, but it's not a good idea to go too big. Like too much text, it can be hard to take in and this defeats the purpose of a mind map. When making a mind map on paper, A4 paper size is just right.

If your mind map is going to be bigger, split it up into two or more mind maps. You may want to create one mind map that's general and covers the basics, and then create supporting mind maps for each of the main points.

## Use Colour and Graphics with Caution

As mentioned, colour coding and graphics are great for mind maps. However, they're only good if they're appropriate and helpful. If you go too crazy with visuals, you may end up with a mind map that's obscure and confusing. Add visuals, but make sure they serve a purpose and enhance the mind map's main ideas.

## The Wrong Tools

Don't use the first mind mapping tool that you come across. It's fun to play around with mind map software programs, but when it's time to get serious, shop around and find a good one that really suits your needs. There are many out there, so do your due diligence. Please see the resources chapter for a list of the top recommended programs.

## Consider Your Audience

Make your mind map with your audience in mind. If it's only for you, this isn't a problem. But if you plan to show your mind map to others or use it in a team situation, make sure it communicates your ideas effectively. Be prepared to explain it if your audience is unfamiliar with mind maps or confused by yours.

## The Map Making Labyrinth

Finally, don't get lost in the process of making mind maps and end up not taking action. Remember that you're creating maps for a reason. Mind mapping can be so fun and addictive that you can make map after map and then never use them.

If you would like to learn step-by-step how mind maps could help you, please take a look at my workshop on mind maps.

Available at www. allthingswriting.com.au/online-training-programs

## Mind map Worksheet

If you prefer mind mapping to outlining, here is an example you can use. You can of course free-form your own, or use mind mapping software.

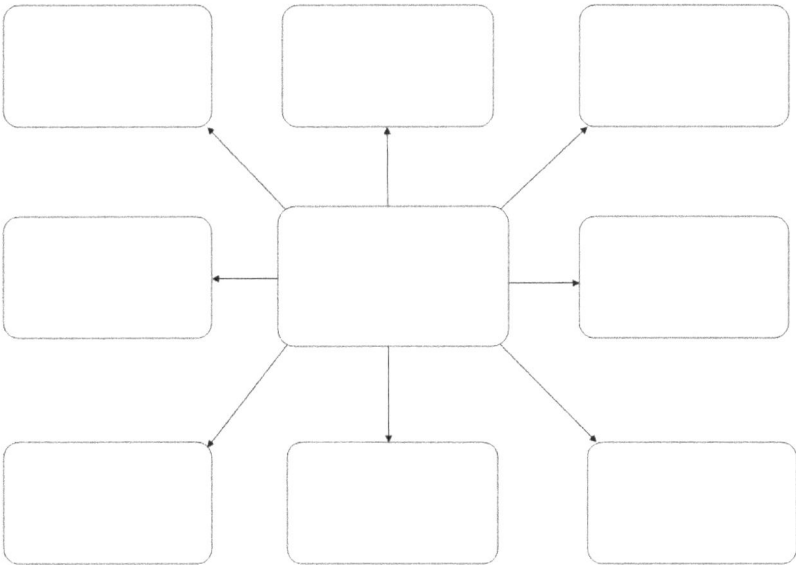

# Chapter Eight

# Ready, Set, GO!

*"The secret to a great book is focus and writing with passion to your audience"*

You've overcome the first hurdle of writing a book – the outline. Now it's time to turn your hard work into a first (rough) draft. The first draft of your book will likely be far different than the finished version, but going through this process will help you weed out what doesn't belong in your masterpiece – and more importantly, what does belong and, what makes it flow.

This process will have you turning your outline into real sentences and paragraphs. It's like painting a picture. In the outline you actually outlined the vision you wanted to create. Now, you're ready to fill in the colours and more detail and make that picture come alive.

Here are 10 basic tips for turning your outline into a first draft:

1. **Simply write!** The bare bones of your first draft will become the flesh and sinew of a real book. Most great writers begin the rough draft of their books by simply writing what first comes to mind. You can always revise and fix problems later. For now, simply write down the bare bones.

2. **Glance at the outline for guidance**. If you become stuck while you're writing, glance at the outline to keep you on track. You may want to keep on writing without looking at the outline – and that's okay too. Whatever works for you! There is no right or wrong.

3. **Before you sit down to write, follow a routine**. Routines are meant to set up our minds before doing something. Drinking a cup of tea, meditating or listening to music may be just the routine you need to get the creative juices flowing.

4. **It's okay to leave gaps**. The purpose of the rough draft is to get your thoughts down when you have time to write or when thoughts come into your mind. There will be words you can't think of and sentences that don't work. Leave them alone, knowing you'll revisit them later and have the answers.

5. **Don't stress about writing**. You'll write much better and your information will flow more smoothly if

you're not stressed about the writing process. Focus on the ideas, not the grammar or structure of your sentences.

**6. Begin anywhere each time you write**. If you're not feeling the urge to write about the subject matter in the first chapter of your book, begin with another chapter you do feel like writing about. Your writing will be much stronger and you'll make more progress.

**7. Keep on writing**. Similar to the first tip, keep on writing means that you continue with the writing process without stopping to go back over what you've already written. It's so tempting to correct and revise your rough draft as you go, but that's not the purpose of the rough draft, and that can keep you from progressing.

**8. Don't procrastinate**. Procrastination is a bad habit that has no place in a writer's world. When you begin to put off the writing process of your book, you're choosing to view it as work, rather than a task to be cherished. If you don't enjoy writing your book, you may have chosen the wrong subject.

**9. Don't edit yourself**. Your first attempt at a rough draft may look like it was written by a first grader. Don't worry about it. If you make a habit of going back to read and edit or rewrite before you finish the draft, you'll never make it to the end.

**10. Leave gaps for later**. You may not have all the facts for your first draft – nor be able to think of words you want to say, but just keep writing. Later, there will be a chance to review and revise. You may want to make an "informational" note to yourself on the draft as a reminder to get the fact or to rephrase the wording.

## Enjoy the Writing Process

Sometimes you have to stop and remember why you wanted to write a book in the first place. You have a story to tell or you wouldn't have thought of writing a book, so keep that in mind during the entire writing process; think about your "why".

The rough draft should be fun, because you're not worried about semantics of how the book should look or read at this time. Write as if you're telling a story to someone who wants to hear it and keep in mind what you're trying to get across.

Most writers keep files or journals full of notes, clippings, references and other memory jogging notes and articles that will help to keep the book interesting and real. When you get an idea during the time you're not at your desk writing, be sure to have a notepad and pen on hand to jot it down. (Of course, many now use the help of an iPhone or iPad for that purpose.)

If you don't like the thought of sitting at a computer typing up your book, you always have the option of recording your thoughts and then getting your book transcribed. This is quite useful if you want your book to have your own personal voice attached to your book. Some people simply have the gift of writing the way they speak.

## Finding your Voice

It is important to find your own voice when writing and many people need help around understanding how to find their voice. Following are 5 tips to help you:

1. Describe yourself in three adjectives. An example would be: fun, helpful, and energetic

2. Ask and answer the question: "Is this how I talk?"

3. Imagine your ideal reader, describe them in detail, write for them and only them

4. Find around three books, articles or blogs that you like to read and take a look at them. Once you are finished, answer the following questions: How are they alike, how are they different, and how does the writing of each of them intrigue you. In most cases we admire what we wish to aspire to

5. Read something that you have already written and take a good look at it. Then ask yourself "Is this something that I would read?" If you answer no, then you need to change your voice

The reason you need to find your voice is key to getting dedicated followers that love the way you write, if you are not being yourself, you will eventually exhaust your writing.

Once you do find your voice, you need to keep developing it. It's a discipline that shouldn't be overlooked, especially if you're going to have the impact you desire with your words.

It's really important to remember that there are many authors out there in the world and if you want to be heard, you need to do a lot more than raise your voice. You must set yourself apart from everyone else and show people that you have something special to say and a very unique way of saying it!

## Which Font and Size Should you use for your book?

The font and size in your book needs to be clear and easy to read for your readers. The best way is to type up a few paragraphs in different fonts and print them out, remember that it looks different on your computer screen. If your book is going to be printed as well as being on Kindle, then you need to consider this closely.

Make sure you do not select a font that is too common or too weird. Following are some recommendations to help you:

Good serif fonts (these are for the interior of your book):

- Hoefler Text
- Sabon
- Georgia
- Minion Pro
- Century (not century gothic)
- Garamond (not ITC garamond)
- Caslon Pro
- Bembo

Good sans serf fonts (used sparingly for contrast in your book):

- Avenir
- Trade gothic
- Helvetica Neue
- Franklin gothic
- News gothic
- Myriad

The worst two fonts to use are: Comic Sans and Papyrus.

The font size most commonly used is 12 for the body copy of your book, 14 for your chapter sub topics, and 16 for your chapter titles.

# Chapter Nine

## Don't Judge a Book By its Cover

*"The cover of your book is the first impression of you that you need to nail in a split second"*

## What's In A Name?

How do you come up with a great book title? This is really important to get right. The best way to do this is to do some research.

The best place to do this is on Amazon, Kindle and iTunes book store. Searching Google is another place to see what keywords people are searching for. This will help you tremendously. When you start to type in your keywords, Google instantly gives you a drop down of phrases to choose from, take careful note of these because this is what people are typing into Google when they are searching, therefore, Google is giving you what is trending most!

Simply go to these websites and search for the topic your book is about. Take a careful look at what they have for their titles, do they stand out or are they boring?

Make sure you select the books that are best sellers, remember they are there for a reason! Take some time here and see what titles or keywords stand out for you. Open up a blank word document and copy these into your document to reference once you have a few gathered.

From the list of titles you have copied, take a look at different ones and look at how you could use some of the words in these titles. Remember to never directly copy what someone else has, this could land you in strife. Mix and match the words to come up with your own awesome title.

Following are some headlines that can help you create your book cover title:

## Question-Style Headlines

1. Are You Ready to Get Serious About [Job/Product/Task]?

2. What Would You Do If You Became a Millionaire in Just One Year? If You Get [Your Product], You Might Just Have the Answer to that Question.

3. Do You Know the Secrets to [Hobby/Profession/Task]? Find Out What You've Been Missing.

4. Your Co-Workers Know Something You Don't. Are You Ready to Learn the Truth?

5. Is Your Business Living Up to Its Potential? Find Out Why It Might Not Be.

6. Are You Ready to Transform Your Hum-Drum Life into a More Positive, Successful, Worthwhile One?

7. Are You Sick and Tired of [Problem #1] and [Problem #2] Preventing You From Achieving [Goal]?

8. Do You Feel Like Progress is Elusive? Like You're Running on a Hamster's Wheel? Find

Out How to Move Forward in [Profession/Business/Hobby].

9.  Are You Prepared to Take Your Future into Your Own Hands?

10. Do You Know That Two Tiny Problems Could Be Killing Your [Business/Love-Life/Career]?

## Benefit-Style Headlines

1.  Learn the Top Five Things that Science Suggests You Should Do to Become Successful at [Career/Business].

2.  Use My Tested Methods for [Achieving Goal #1] and [Achieving Goal #2] in Just Days!

3.  Finally Experience the Benefits of Using a Real, Effective, Authentic [Type of Product].

4.  There's an Important Difference Between [Your Product] and All Others: [State Biggest Benefit of Your Product].

5.  Change Your Life Overnight with [Name of Your Product]!

6.  Improve Your Energy-Levels, Get Healthier, and Enjoy Your Life to its Fullest Using My Proven Strategies

7. Steal My Ideas to Make Your Business More Powerful, Effective, and Better-Monetised

8. It Took Me [# of Years] Years to Learn This. But You Can Learn It In as Little as [# of Days] Days.

9. Sick of the Rat Race? Find Out How to Get Out of Your Cage Using My Patented Strategies for Being Successful in [Name of Niche].

10. Tired of Your Lackluster Ability to [What Product Does]? Make the Switch to [Your Product] and Change Everything in Just Days!

## How-To Style Headlines

1. Learn How to Change Your Life and Your Career in Just [# of Days] Days Using My Proven System.

2. Don't Despair. Find Out How to Explode Your Profits in Just [# of Steps] Simple Steps.

3. Find Out How Other, Ordinary People Just Like You Become Wildly Successful at [Career/Hobby/Task].

4. Learn How to Triple The Amount of Traffic That Comes to Your Site in Just [# of Days] Days.

5. Learn How to Transform Your [Career/Hobby/Relationship] in Just [# of Days] Days and [# of Steps] Steps!

6. Learn How the Experts Do Things. Adopt My Proven System to Change How You Do [Whatever Your Product Promises].

7. How to Build an Empire from the Ashes of Your Failed Business Venture

8. How to Improve Your Relationship with Your [Spouse/Kids/Family] without Hurting Your [Career/Other Goal]

**Trigger Word Style Headlines**

1. Seven Explosive Secrets that are Guaranteed to [Product's Promise]

2. Sick of Paying Outrageous Amounts for [Niche Product]? Download Your Copy for Free.

3. You Might Be Shocked to Learn What Science Has to Say About [Niche]

4. Warning: If You Think Your Business Practices Are Good Enough, "You Might be in For an Unpleasant Surprise"

5. The Fast Win Big and the Slow Fade Over Time. Learn Why The Coming Revolution in [Your Niche] Might Render Your Business [Slow].

6. The World is Changing Around You. Adjust to the Times or Face Extinction. Read On to Learn How [Your Business/Your Career/Your Family Life] Will Change... Forever.

7. Learn the 10 Dangerous Secrets that Every Successful Person in [Your Niche/Career] Knows, But You Don't

8. Generate a Hurricane of Revenue in [Niche] Using These Secret Strategies that Even Some of the Best [People in Your Niche/Business] Don't Know

Following is a template to jot down your title ideas:

## Title Ideas Page

You have a working title, but maybe it's not working hard enough? List other title possibilities as they come to you, then come back and review them with fresh eyes later.

_____

_____

_____

_____

Once you have done your research and got some title ideas, combine these and layout your book title page in the space provided:

## Book Title Page

Title: Subtitle: Author: Website: Publisher:

# Sell To The World - Creating Your Book Cover

Congratulations! You have finally finished writing your book. You are breathing a huge sigh of relief, I am sure you are feeling quite proud of yourself, if you aren't, you should be. This is not something everyone achieve's, many people want to and don't, so WELL DONE, I am proud of you!!

The next step is to create the cover of your book.

Following are 7 excellent tips to create your book cover PLUS a golden rule:

1. **Membership** - Your book cover should be about membership, not aesthetics. Therefore, it does not have to be beautiful or interesting. What it does need is to let people know exactly what genre your book belongs in. Your book needs to look like it belongs, don't stress about it looking like all the others, it is much better to be selling your book than to stand out and sell no copies at all.

2. **Lust Factor** - If this is your very first book and you are going to design it yourself or outsource it inexpensively, it is very important that your cover has

the lust factor! It really is important to not miss the opportunity of making sure your book cover is awesome and gets noticed easily, so please make sure you get a professional to take care of this, it might cost you a little more, however the end results will be worth it.

3. **The blink test** - No matter which cover you chose, the most important thing to remember is that your book cover needs to tell people what it's about in a split second. Ask yourself, "Does it communicate the genre immediately?" Your book cover is not the place to explain all the details about your book, people simply won't read all the text on your cover unless they have been captured by the cover alone in that split second. It needs to attract, appeal, and communicate the basics and have an immediate emotional impact.

4. **The title is integral** - Your book needs to have a great title. It is best to work out your title before you get the cover design done because book covers have to compensate. If you were to pick a one word title that was simple or abstract, it won't say much about the book, which means the cover design will need to all the work. Otherwise, you could have a very long keyword rich descriptive title, which would mean the cover design, does not need to be doing much of the work to sell it.

5. **Taglines or subtitles** - These are used by many people to explain a not so good title. If your title and cover design is great, you won't need a tagline to add more information, hence people are unlikely to read the small text on your book anyway in this instance. Many first time publishers miss this great opportunity and put titles that don't make sense, they have bad book covers and they don't add any small text, so in turn they don't pass the 'blink test'. All self published authors need to have a great title and subtitle or perhaps a small blurb on the cover that gives more information so that it passes the blink test.

6. **Consider your distribution platform** - If Amazon is your primary sales platform, which they are unless you are a professional speaker or you are planning to sell thousands of copies at events, then you need to design your cover for Amazon. Your book cover will show as a thumbnail size, so think about this for a minute, also realise that people don't read text on thumbnails! This means your cover needs to stand out and be very impactful so that people will click on the image to find out more.

7. **Hierarchy** - If you are a first time author you will not have a platform, so the title of your book should not be your name. Your title should be 100% and fill the width of your book cover. Your author name should be

50%. Don't feel like your name should be in small print because you are not yet famous. Your author name should be at the minimum the same size as others in your genre.

**The Golden Rule** - "Be Clear Before You Are Clever". Many authors want to be creative and make an impression, they want to refer to the contents of the book - remember this is a book people haven't read yet! People will not understand what you are referring to, so don't try and be clever.

Remember not to use a shortened version of words, like 'Biz' (instead of Business) or mis-spelling of words as this will definitely lose you sales.

The cover of your book packaging is a billboard. It is there to catch the eye and attract people to read the summary and reviews. That's it. Make a beautiful cover that sells the book. Please don't get caught up in all the stuff that does not matter. The best book cover is the cover that sells the most books!

The colour of your book cover is very important. For more information, please take a look at the "Psychology of Colour".

## Front Book Cover

Use this page to lay out your idea for a book cover. Think about title, subtitle, and author name placement, any images you want to include, etc.

# Daily Strengths for Daily Needs

It is highly recommended that you include images in your book. Please remember that you cannot simply take images you see on the internet and use them unless you have permission. This could lead you into copyright issues, so please purchase your images or use your own images. There are royalty free images that you can get, however, it is really important to make sure you check that they are fully royalty free, in some instances they are not.

Below are some resources on where you can purchase images:

- Photodune.net
- Dreamstime.com
- istockphoto.com

- Gettyimages.com.au
- Fotolia.com
- Shutterstock.com
- Bigstockphoto.com

Another aspect that you could add to your book is quotes. Depending on the book you are writing of course will determine what your quotes will be. The best quotes to use are your own, the reason is that you are taking the reader away from you and promoting someone else.

However, if you are happy to include quotes from other people, then simply go onto Google and type in for example: 'inspirational quotes'. Please see the resources chapter for more information and links.

A note on using quotes in your book, if you are going to use other peoples quotes, please make sure that you credit the person that wrote the quote, again you need to adhere to copyright laws.

## Words That Sell

The back cover of your book is crucial and must be done carefully and precisely, especially if you want to sell your book! Many authors rush this part and almost always get it wrong, please don't do that, take your time. Many people think it's just the back of the book, how important can it be? The answer is VERY important.

The 150 to 200 words that you put on the back cover of your book is the most important words you will write in your entire book. The reason is because after people look at the book title and front cover, the next thing they look at is the back cover, this is where they decide whether they will purchase your book.

The cover of your book also functions as the primary ad for your book, not only will it appear on your book, but you will most likely use it as your description that appears on Amazon.

The reason you only have around 150 to 200 words is because that is what will fit best on most back covers without having to reduce the size of the font, which would make it hard to read and that would in turn not help you with sales!

Before you attempt to write your back cover, do some research and see what others have written in the same genre for examples of how it should be done.

If your book is a novel, your back cover should provide a short summary of what your book is about. Only write one or two paragraphs that include hooks, by that I mean some of the story's most engaging plot points.

Remember to end your description with an intriguing question or a point of tension, something that will hook the reader on the book's premise or the character's main dilemma. Don't go into great detail here, the aim is to sell the readers on the big picture narrative.

If you are writing a non-fiction book you should make a list of bullet points about the book's main features and actually put that list on the back cover. Use three to five bullet points only, market research shows that an odd number works best.

In your bullet points, tell your reader what the book will do for them or what they are going to learn from your book.

It is important to keep the syntax (style) of your bullet points consistent. This is very important as your list won't read right otherwise. If you start out with participles, stick with participles (a participle is a form of a verb that is used in a sentence to modify a noun, noun phrase, verb, or verb phrase, and thus plays a role similar to that of an adjective or adverb. It is one of the types of nonfinite verb forms); if you start with clauses, then please stick with clauses (in grammar, a clause is the smallest grammatical unit that can express a complete proposition. A typical clause consists of a subject and a predicate, where the predicate is typically a verb phrase - a verb together with any objects and other modifiers).

Following are some examples of inconsistent bullet points:

In this book you'll learn that:

- A cat can be litterbox-trained in a day

- Feeding the right kind of diet

- How to stop behaviour problems

Now for an example of consistent bullet points:

In this book, you'll learn how to:

- Litterbox-train your cat in a day

- Feed your cat a proper diet that extends life of your cat

- Stop behaviour problems in their tracks

Can you see the difference between the two? The first one sounds like an amateur wrote it, where the second one sounds much better and flows well.

Your bullet list should appear in the middle of your copy that you write. Above the list you should be speaking directly to your readers, making sure that you give them a primary reason why they should be reading your book. This needs to be a bit more broad in it's scope than the reasons in your bulleted list. One way you could write this primary reason is by asking a question.

It is important that you make your readers the focus not yourself. Tell them why they should trust what you have to say. This is where you really need to get in touch with your reader's *need* for the book, and *strike a chord* with that, otherwise they will walk away never even opening the pages of your book, no matter how awesome your writing or content is.

## Your Bio and Picture

Once you have carefully crafted your back cover content, it's now time to include a professional photo of you, the author. This should be a clean, clear close up photo of your face, make sure nothing else is in this photo.

Next step is to write a brief bio that includes two or three points that establishes you as the expert with the training and/or experience that qualifies you to write about this topic in your book. This bio is not the same as the one you include in the inside pages of your book, that particular bio should be a page that appears near the back of your book where it covers information about you in more detail.

## What Not To Say On The Back Cover

Basically, anything that we have discussed so far. Remember, you only have 150 to 200 words to reach your audience, make sure you keep it short and focused. Make sure you cut out anything that is repetitious so you can cram in as much information as you can into those few hundred words.

An important point to remember is to make sure your tone is understated. People know and understand that you have written this back cover as an ad for your book, so if you write about it in superlatives, it will only make you look bad, people will think you are arrogant, desperate, or exaggerating.

To overcome this, simply write with confidence whilst being humble, stating the facts of the book and telling them what the benefits are, this will always win you trust rather than ridicule.

If you have endorsements, especially ones that are recognised in your market or genre, then this would be a great place to add them. If you take a look at some back covers, you will see that all they have is endorsements! If you have a few of these, then that is all you need for your back cover content. When you have well known people that give you endorsements, then you need to let people know, this alone will sell your book!

Following is a template to layout and write your back cover:

## Back Book Cover

Design the back cover for your book. Brief description, author bio, bullet points, etc.

# Tying Up Loose Ends

Other pages you can include where you deem it necessary include a 'Terms of Use', 'Income Disclaimer, Liability Disclaimer', and 'Copyright' information into your book. I have included a copy of what I have in some of my books, please feel free to use them, however, I take no responsibility if you do use them.

You also need to apply for an 'EIN' number if you want to sell your book on Amazon in the United States of America. The EIN is your tax number that is required, especially if you do not want to pay the full tax amount.

**Terms of Use**

You are given a non-transferable, "personal use" license to this book. You cannot distribute it or share it with other individuals.

Also, there are no resale rights or private label rights granted when purchasing this book. In other words, it's for your own personal use only.

**Income Disclaimer**

This book contains strategies, methods and other advice that, regardless of my own results and experience, may not produce the same results (or any results) for you. I make absolutely no guarantee, expressed or implied, that by following the advice below you will make any headway or improve your current situation, as there are several factors and variables that come into play regarding any given method.

Primarily, results will depend on the nature of your lifestyle, the condition of your lifestyle, the experience of the individual, situations and elements that are beyond your control.

As with any endeavour, you assume all risk related to the results based on your own discretion and at your own potential input.

**Liability Disclaimer**

By reading this book, you assume all risks associated with using the advice given below, with a full understanding that you, solely, are responsible for anything that may occur as a result of putting this information into action in any way, and regardless of your interpretation of the advice.

You further agree that our company cannot be held responsible in any way for the success or failure of your outcomes as a result of the information presented below. It is your responsibility to conduct your own due diligence regarding the safe and successful operation of your lifestyle if you intend to apply any of our information in any way to your life.

## Copyright

## Applying for your EIN

It is very important that you apply for an EIN (Employee Independent Number) before you sell any of your books online. The EIN is the number you require that will save you paying the highest tax rate applicable.

Please follow the instructions below for applying to get your EIN:

Call the IRS at 0011 1 267 941 1099

This is a direct line to the dedicated unit in Philadelphia that deals with foreign entities (that's you) who need an EIN.

Press 2 on the computerised menu to get through to an operator. While I've heard it's possible to get your EIN through some embassies and consuls, that certainly doesn't apply to all of them and this number will work for *everyone.*

Note: they won't take a call from anyone using a "speakerphone". If you are using Skype on your laptop, have a set of headphones plugged in before you call, to avoid an undignified scramble around your environment. Finally, while there is an online facility for doing this, foreign entities *can't* use that.

1. Tell them you're applying for an EIN for a foreign entity.

They may ask if you are the legal officer of the company or similar, I said that I was a sole proprietor, and the owner of the business, which satisfied them.

2. There's a 50% chance that they will tell you that you need Form SS-4 .

You do not want to go down this path, this requires form-filling, fees, delays. If this is what they tell you, politely end the call, and call them back. I only had to do this once, and then got someone a little more helpful.

3. Give your details

They will ask for your name, mailing address, phone number, the name of your company, and the country it was incorporated. This will involve a lot of spelling and repetition, but make sure all the details are correct.

4. They will ask if this is for compliance with withholding. Say "yes".

5. They will ask if you have a social security number, green card, ITIN or if you have filled in any forms. Say "no"

6. They will ask if this is for e-books, Say "yes".

7. They will give you your EIN!!!

After confirming all your details, they will give you your EIN right there and then. Resist the urge to shower your helpful IRS employee with virtual kisses.

Also, it's probably best not to try and sell them your book!

Write your EIN down, somewhere safe, then save it on your computer, upload it to Dropbox, copy it to a thumb drive, email it to yourself, carve it on the biggest tree in your garden, and consider getting it tattooed somewhere private! That is how precious this number is!

## ISBN

Your ISBN (International Standard Book Number) is a unique numeric commercial book identifier. This is the number and barcode you see on the back of book covers.

There are two options for getting your ISBN.

First, you can get one from Createspace. The downside of this is that the ownership does not lie with you, it is with Createspace. Sometimes 'free' doesn't work in your favour!

Secondly, and the best option is to purchase your own. One resource is http://www.myidentifiers.com where you can simply buy one or a block of 10, I recommend a block of 10 as it is cheaper in the long run.

## Create Front Matter and Back Matter

Apart from the pages I just mentioned, you need to decide what other pages you want in the front and back of your book. Some options are as follows:

**Front Matter:**

- Title Page

- Copyright Page

- Dedication

- Table of Contents

- Foreword

- Preface

- Acknowledgements

Following is a template to include which of the following pages you are going to include in your book:

# Front Matter Page

*Title Page ~ Copyright ~ Dedication ~ Table of Contents ~ Acknowledgments ~ Preface ~ Foreword*

**Back Matter:**

- Afterword

- Appendix

- About the Author

- Other Call to Action (e.g. other books)

- Coming Soon

Following is a template to include which of the following pages you are going to include in your book:

## Back Matter Page

*Afterword ~ Coming Soon ~ Appendix ~ About the Author ~ Other Call to Action (eg. Other books)*

# Chapter Ten

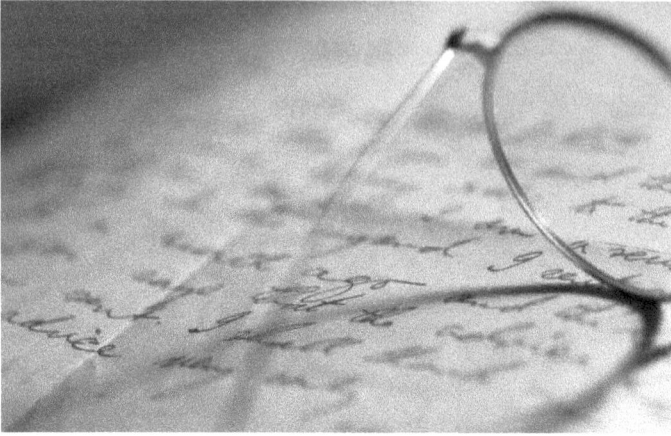

# Eliminating Embarrassing Writing Errors

*"Proofreading and editing is boring…yet it is the most crucial part of your book that you need to get right"*

This is the polishing phase of your book. After the rough draft is complete in its sketchy form, you need to go back, reread, review and revise what you've got so far.

During the revision phase, you'll be fixing more than simple misspellings and commas in your draft. You'll be taking a fresh look from a critical viewpoint and honing your book so that it will be transformed from crude grammar and gaping holes to a refined and well-thought-out book to present for publishing.

You'll be scrutinising your draft to see if what you've done so far is exactly what you wanted to say and in the method you want to say it (for example, with enough humour and detail) and targeted to the proper audience.

The process of reviewing and revising your rough draft into a final product is important and if you've never done it before, there are some things you should know that will make the task easier, faster and more productive.

**Editing and Proofreading**

You're approaching the finish line of completing your book when you reach the editing and proofreading stage. Editing your draft includes looking for phrases you can make more forceful and avoiding repetition within the book.

Proofreading is looking for commas and other grammar faux paux that can make a difference in how your readers comprehend what you're trying to say. At this level of book polishing, it's best to read the manuscript aloud so you can get the full impact of the words and the punctuation choices you've made.

**Proof Reading Techniques**

- Slowly read your document aloud.

- Read your report backwards.

- Read one word at a time (for typos, spelling errors, etc).

- Re-read.

- NOTE: Spell check will not catch everything, and grammar checks are often wrong!

## Get Others to Read Your Document

Don't be the only proofreader! As a writer, you will be inclined to miss inconsistencies or errors because you can anticipate what you mean to say. Therefore, arrange for people to check what you have written.

For an important document you will need a person to check it for accuracy. Then get someone with a keen eye for checking typos, spelling and grammar.

Remember that not everyone is equally good at both these tasks; so you may need to arrange for two people to help. Offer to return the favour.

## Proof Reading Exercise

There are more than 32 errors in the following passage. Can you spot them?

- At some time or other we all have to pleed guilty to unthikningly using buzz words and hackneyed phrases. Of course, what greats with one person may inpress another. But some express-ions unequivocally point to a lazy or carless writer Repeat offenders are 'at this point in time', 'moving forward, 'I hear what you are saying', etc, etc. And all those football locker-room phrases like 'levelplaying field', 'shifting the gaolposts', 'dropping the ball' - and so on... and on, A recent habitt is the the over-use of 'pasionate' - as in the job advertiusment seeking aplicants who are 'passionate' about goods recievable clerical work'. (Are you serious?) So, let's all be a littlte more consious about the words and phrases we use. Please...

## Editing Techniques

So much of good writing is in the editing – so take it seriously. Review these later in order of concerns:

- Spelling

- Punctuation

- Sentence structure

- Writing style

- Presentation

## Editing Exercise

Rewrite these phrases and clauses more simply. If you think they are superfluous, cross them out.

1. In order that

   _____

2. It is my understanding

   _____

3. It is indeed unfortunate

   _____

4. In the near future

   _____

5. At this point of time

   _____

6. It has been stated herein

   _____

7. It is our opinion

   _____

8.  It is worthy of repetition

    _____

9.  I believe the plan will meet with successful attainment

    _____

10. Activation of this policy should terminate the situation

    _____

11. It may be said without fear of contradiction

    _____

12. There is generally

    _____

13. There are many instances where

    _____

14. He had a sales background in real estate

    _____

15. Implementation is proceeding in accordance with instructions

_____

16. These machines have excellent high-speed product capacity

_____

17. Due to the fact that

_____

18. In addition to this

_____

19. It is repeated again

_____

20. The reason why is because

_____

21. Do any other superfluous or loose phrases come to mind?

_____

## Advanced Editing Exercise

These exercises are designed to help you discover whether any aspects of your writing are in need of improvement. Note the main faults in the following sentences, and then rewrite the sentences correctly. If you think they are satisfactory as they are, say so.

1.  The errors which we have listed are examples of errors which occur frequently and which should have been discovered immediately.

    _____
    _____
    _____
    _____
    _____

2.  Having decided what procedures to adopt, the drafting of a new manual is undertaken.

    _____
    _____
    _____
    _____
    _____

3. We make the following recommendation for the utilisation of the advantages of mechanisation.

_____
_____
_____
_____
_____

4. The survey should include those women who are unhappy with our products and their husbands and children.

_____
_____
_____
_____
_____

5. Every effort should be made to get rid of the five per cent of our work force involved in accidents.

_____
_____
_____
_____
_____

6.  If you buy now, you can have two per cent.

    _____
    _____
    _____
    _____
    _____

7.  Neither the file copy, nor the original, which was posted two months earlier, were found.

    _____
    _____
    _____
    _____
    _____

8.  As analyses such as was requested in your letter are essential prerequisites to effective decision making, I hope you will find the following suggestions as useful to you.

    _____
    _____
    _____
    _____
    _____

9.  Your signature, as well as those of two witnesses, are required.

    _____
    _____
    _____
    _____
    _____

10. This campaign was conducted to reduce the number of poorly written reports during the year, which was successful.

    _____
    _____
    _____
    _____
    _____

11. These are background information, which should only have been in a paragraph or two, if at all.

    _____
    _____
    _____
    _____
    _____

12. Each officer responsible should approve orders for purchases for his department which he has made.

_____

_____

_____

_____

_____

## Time to Hire a Professional Editor

After you're as sure as you can be that your book is polished and finished, think about hiring a professional editor to pronounce it "finished." You can try to get a recommendation for an editor through another writer or a professional publisher.

Before you choose an editor, be sure they can provide samples of their work and that they have references. Although the editor likely won't be savvy enough to know all the facts you're writing about, they can make recommendations on glaring mistakes and style.

Remember that you don't have to take everyone's feedback as law. Make your own decisions on some feedback issues, but take every one of them seriously so that you can feel confident as you progress to the publishing stage of your masterpiece.

# Your Publishing Friend

Congratulations! You've put the final touches on your book and it's ready for publishing. You can call yourself a writer – and be proud of the long (and sometimes excruciating) process you went through to write your book. Now it's time to get it published.

## Digital Self-Publishing Methods

Many new authors are making their marks on the book publishing world that would never have been "discovered" before the internet gave us such self-publishing options as Createspace and Kindle (KDP) – two of the most popular digital self-publishing methods. Here are some features of each that you might want to consider:

**CreateSpace** – This Independent Publishing site can get you published right away and start the royalties coming in rather than waiting for an agent to find the right publishing house for your book.

With the free download, you get such tools as a cover creator, reviewer and an image gallery from which to choose images for your book. CreateSpace also offers services such as editing, design and marketing.

Unlike brick and mortar publishing houses, your work is published to meet the demand with CreateSpace, so your title is always available and there's no inventory cost.

You may also reach other readers through Amazon, Kindle and other distribution options that CreateSpace makes available – plus, you can create your own eStore quickly and easily.

**Kindle** – Kindle Direct Publishing has turned the publishing world upside down with its ability to reach millions of readers with instant access and a publishing process that takes less than 5 minutes and that has your book on the "shelves" within 24 to 48 hours.

When you choose Amazon's Kindle for your publishing and distribution needs, you'll earn up to 70% royalty on each and every sale and they also offer KDP Select that lets you earn even more through the lending library and Kindle Unlimited.

You'll also keep control of your own rights and are able to set your own prices. You may also make changes to your book as many times and as often as you like.

## Advantages of Being a Published Author

Authors are respected and revered by just about everyone. Their books are proof that they accomplished something that most people never will – a feat akin to reaching the top of Mount Everest. Aside from the respect and adoration people hold for authors, there are a multitude of other benefits a published author can expect. Among them are:

- **Credibility** – By publishing a book, you're establishing yourself as an expert on the subject you wrote about and now have the authority to speak about the subject.

- **Value to your career path** – You can add more value to your employment possibilities when you write a book about your experiences or knowledge in your field of excellence.

- **Increase business** – If you have an online business or any type of business, writing a book can make people want to do business with you.

- **Respect** – The ability to say you are a published author will gain respect from others for what you've gone through and accomplished.

Perhaps the most wonderful benefit you get from writing and publishing a book is the huge boost of self-confidence and pride you experience from actually accomplishing what you set out to do. You'll gain a sense of belief in yourself that few people have when you see your book as a finished product. Surely, you'll want to begin another book right away and you'll be enthused about the process – because now you know what writing is all about.

Perhaps Enid Bagnold, a highly successful writer of plays and movies in the 1940s (National Velvet and The Chalk Garden were just two of her works) said it best about becoming a writer:

"Who wants to become a writer? Why become a writer? Because it's the answer to everything…it's the streaming reason for living. To note, to pin down, to build up, to create, to be astonished at nothing, to cherish the oddities, to let nothing go down the drain, to make something, to make a great flower out of life, even if it's a cactus."

## Lift Off!!

Once you have finished writing your book, it's time to upload it to Createspace. If you have written your book in "Word", make sure you export your book as a PDF as mentioned earlier. If you have written your book using Scrivener, it's time to compile it and export it as a PDF for Createspace or a .mobi for Kindle.

Many aspects of the self-publishing process can be intimidating and confusing, especially the first time you do them. Gone are the days where you need to buy thousands of copies of your book only to have them collect dust in the garage. Following is a step-by-step guide to the process of publishing your book with Createspace. This is a great way to get your book done quickly, easily and you only have to purchase one copy if that is all you want!

Signing up with CreateSpace is easy. Go to their website https://www.createspace.com/ and open an account. You'll receive a member ID number and access to your dashboard. Your dashboard will look something like this, minus my blacked out information.

1. Click the blue **Add New Title** button. This takes you to the **Start Your New Project** page.

2. On the **Start Your New Project** page, fill in the name of your book, the type of project and choose a setup method.

There are two choices:

1. **Guided:** A step-by-step process with directions along the way.

2. **Expert:** A streamlined single-page experience for those familiar with the process.

3. Click the **Get Started** button by your choice and move on to the next step.

4. Title Information page: Fill in your book title, subtitle (if applicable), author name,

contributors, series name and number (if applicable) and other details.

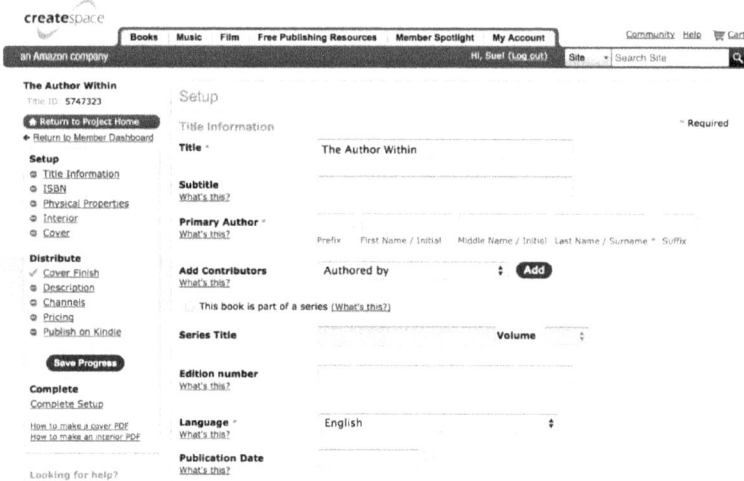

**Note:** If you leave **Publication Date** blank, the date your book publishes on Createspace will be added. If you published the book previously on Kindle for instance or with a traditional publisher, you can fill in the original published date if you wish.
Click **Save & Continue**.

**ISBN:** CreateSpace says, "An ISBN (number) is required to publish and distribute a book." They offer two options. One is free.

**Note:** Compare the options carefully because once you make your choice it cannot be changed. Choose and click **Continue**.

The second choice is to purchase your own (this is highly recommended).

Your ISBN can be purchased from www.myidentifiers.com.

## Interior:

Choose from:

1. black & white or colour (please note that colour will cost you more)
2. paper color (white or cream)
3. trim size (size of your book). The most popular trim size is 6" x 9" – trade paperback size. Createspace does not offer standard paperback size.

4. **Then comes the "fun" part, uploading your book!**

You can either hire a Createspace professional to do it for you, with prices starting at $349, or you can do it yourself.

Following are the do it yourself methods:

- Upload your work as a print-ready .pdf, .doc, .docx, or .rtf file using the templates provided at the back of this book.
- Download a Word® Template, either a blank template or a formatted template with sample content designed for the trim size you choose. I use the formatted 6" x 9" template.

The thumbnails on the left show how a Createspace formatted template is set up. Each pair of pages represents the front and back sides of one printed page. The left page of each pair would actually be the right hand page in a book, while the right one would be on the left (backside of right page).

The midline in each pair represents the outside edge of the page; the left and right borders are the edge of the page that would be bound, forming the book's spine. Because more space is necessary on the bound

edge, the text must be offset closer to the outside edge (the centre line of each pair). See this spacing difference in the illustration above.

There is a table of contents included in the formatted template. If you don't want one in your book, simply delete that pair of pages. You can also delete the dedication and acknowledgements pages if you wish, or you can add pages to the front matter, such as a list of your published books and/or "Praise for" pages with short review excerpts. I place this type of material before the title page as do traditional publishers.

**TIP:** Use section breaks between the elements of your front matter to maintain proper spacing. This also allows you to add page numbers when you come to the body of your story. If you want page numbers in the front matter, use Roman numerals.

Add alternating headers, placing your book title on the right hand pages and your author name on the left. Regarding font styles, the CreateSpace conversion program doesn't recognise all fonts, so it's best to stick to standard ones unless you want to have problems. After you upload your formatted manuscript and it goes through the Createspace automated print check, view your book page by page using the Interior Reviewer. If Createspace catches formatting errors, you will need to fix them and re-upload. This can be time consuming, but you want your baby to look good, right? In case you can't figure out the glitch, email or call CreateSpace Support.

## 5. Cover:

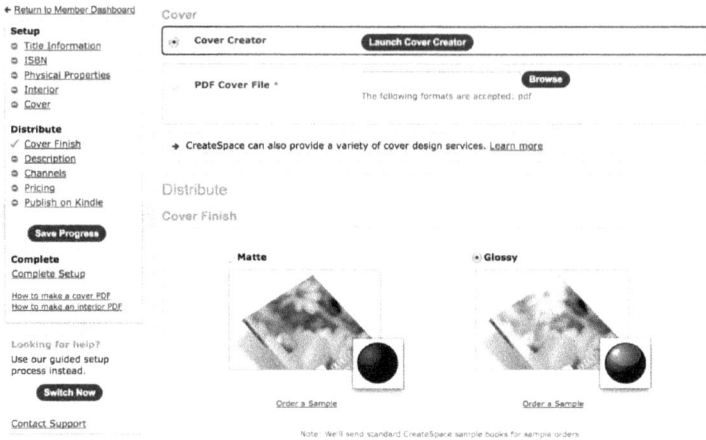

1. Choose a finish for your book cover, either matte or glossy. This is new. Until recently, all covers were glossy.
2. Next, choose how to submit your book cover. There are three methods:
- **Build Your Cover Online with Cover Creator**, a free Createspace tool to design your book covers. (See below)
- **Professional Cover Design**, starting at $399.

- **Upload a Print-Ready PDF Cover:** Createspace provides detailed instructions for this method.

My personal recommendation is to hire a professional

book cover designer that will give you the best results.

Using **Cover Creator:** Choose from several pages of pre-made Createspace cover designs (below on left) or design your own cover using a blank template (on right.)

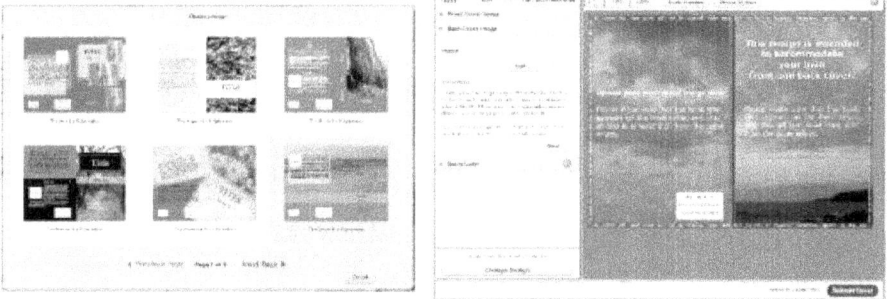

This is a sample template.

1. First, design the front cover (I do this offline) making sure your image has a DPI of at least 300. Anything less than that will be rejected by the Createspace program.

2. After the front cover successfully loads, design the back cover. Include:

   - a short, catchy blurb
   - short review excerpts
   - an author photo

**Note:** You should have already done this, however,

this is a prompt it you haven't.

3. Look at the back of paperback books for ideas, and be careful to leave space for the barcode and trimming, as per Createspace instructions.

4. Lastly, set up the spine.

5. **Complete Setup:** Review your project setup.

If everything looks okay, submit your files for review. You can go back and make changes if you need to. When ready, submit for review.

6. **Review:** The CreateSpace automated review program makes sure your work passes muster for "manufacturing and cataloging". If it does, you will be asked if you want to order a proof copy (at cost) for your final approval. I always do this because there could still be issues that need correcting. When you are satisfied, give Createspace the go-ahead to publish your print book. **Note:** Do the following while waiting for the automated review to be completed (it may take several hours or longer).

7. **Distribution Channels:** Choose distribution channels. Expanded Distribution used to cost $25 but is now FREE!

8. **Pricing:** Set a price for your book. Use the built in calculator to determine what the royalties will be.

Keep in mind that distributors usually discount the book price and Amazon will match the discounted price. If you set your price too low, your proceeds will suffer when the book is discounted. Of course you don't want to price your book so high that it scares off readers.

9. **Description:** Provide a description for your s sales page. Assign a BISAC Category; add your author bio; set language, country of publication; choose search keywords; check for adult content if applicable and if you want use large print.

**The Author Within**

Title ID: 5747323

- ⬆ Return to Project Home
- ← Return to Member Dashboard

**Setup**
- ⊖ Title Information
- ⊖ ISBN
- ⊖ Physical Properties
- ⊖ Interior
- ⊖ Cover

**Distribute**
- ✓ Cover Finish
- ⊖ Description
- ⊖ Channels
- ⊖ Pricing
- ⊖ Publish on Kindle

**Save Progress**

**Complete**

Complete Setup

How to make a cover PDF
How to make an interior PDF

Looking for help?
Use our guided setup
process instead.

**Switch Now**

Contact Support

Pricing

⚠ **ACTION REQUIRED:** You must save your progress and address any outstanding issues before you can set your list price. **Save Progress**

Complete Setup

Review your title setup. If all information is correct, then submit your files for review. We'll ensure your information complies with our submission requirements and e-mail you with next steps.

⊘ **INCOMPLETE:** Title Information must be completed before submitting for review.

⊘ **INCOMPLETE:** ISBN must be completed before submitting for review.

⊘ **INCOMPLETE:** Physical Properties must be completed before submitting for review.

⊘ **INCOMPLETE:** Interior must be completed before submitting for review.

⊘ **INCOMPLETE:** Cover must be completed before submitting for review.

⊘ **INCOMPLETE:** Description must be completed before submitting for review.

⊘ **INCOMPLETE:** Channels must be completed before submitting for review.

⊘ **INCOMPLETE:** Pricing must be completed before submitting for review.

By clicking Submit for Review, you are agreeing to and confirming your compliance with the Member Agreement.

**Save Progress** **Submit for Review**

In conclusion, take your time, follow directions on the site and, if you ever get stuck, contact Createspace support. Their people are courteous and helpful.

## Chapter Eleven

## Connecting The Dots

*"You book is finally complete. The hard work has paid*

*off…You have achieved personal excellence and success"*

### Waiting for Approval of Your Book

Once you have uploaded your book to Createspace, the team there will read your book and make sure that it meets all their criteria. Don't panic, I am sure your book will pass with flying colours. This process does not take too long, depending on their workload it should only take 24 to 48 hours.

## Once Approved

Once your book is approved, you will receive an email from Createspace notifying you that your book is ready for you to proofread. You have two choices:

1. Proofread it online, or

2. Get a hard copy sent to you

If this is your very first book, I highly recommend option 2.

Once you order your book it only takes around 3 to 4 hours to be printed and shipped to you.

## Getting Your Book

This is the most exciting moment in your life; well it was for me anyway! When that book arrives in the post and you have it in your hands, it is the proudest moment and you should revel in it. You deserve it, you have really achieved an awesome step in your life. CONGRATULATIONS!!!

## Proofread Again

Now that you have your book in your hot little hands, it's now the time to proofread it again. This is not such a hard job, however it is very important to make sure your spelling and grammar is all correct, also making sure that the layout of each page is exactly as you want it to look. Make sure that the formatting is all OK. If you have any tables, models or graphs, make sure that they all look good and not out of whack. If you find any changes, make them in your original document that you uploaded to Createspace and upload it again. Once you are happy with the result, submit your book for approval again. Once it is approved, have another quick look at the online version to make sure it is correct. If it all looks good, you are ready to sell your book or purchase them if that is the purpose of your book.

## How to Become a Bestseller

Every author wants to become a best selling author, however many don't know how to achieve this or where to even start! Would you agree that the best way to achieve a goal like this is to follow a proven path? A path that is well defined, well thought out and has been proven to work time and time again?

There are methods, proven methods to becoming a bestselling author that work. There have been many changes in the last 10 years when it comes to selling your book. There are many obstacles that all aspiring authors face, however in my coaching and mentoring program I show you how the process works so you can achieve that Number One Best Seller status!

For more information on my coaching and mentoring program, please contact me at sue@suekennedy.com.au

## Promote Your Expertise Through Various Channels

Now that you have your book, it's time to let people know about it! A great way to do this is by networking.

The most successful business owners will tell you that there are three critical assets in their business and they are:

- Their customers
- Their product or services
- Their business relationships

All of these take hard work to develop, but the third one (business relationships) is one that often gets neglected. Relationships are difficult to build at the best of times. But, when you're busy with all the other "stuff" in life, they're often the part that gets neglected – whether they're personal or business relationships.

## What is Power Networking?

Power networking is a life skill and lifestyle habit. It involves going out in a systematic way and meeting new people in order to build a list of contacts. With power networking, you're meeting people with a clear goal in mind. However, it's not an activity you do only when you want something. It's an ongoing process that creates long-term, mutually beneficial relationships.

## The Power Networking Process

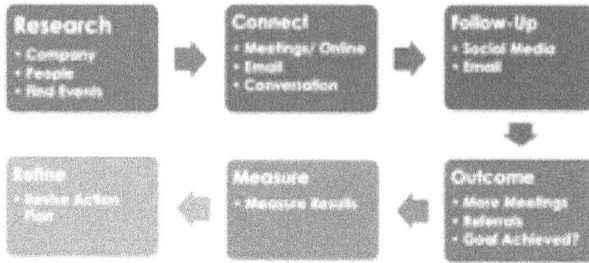

## The Key to Successful Power Networking

In order for your networking to be truly powerful, you need to have a clear purpose in mind. Perhaps it's to promote your book, the services you provide, or maybe you're just building a list of contacts so that when you need something, you can tap into this list. You may also choose to augment your list when you have a new goal that requires new contacts. But with a specific purpose in mind, you'll have a more focused network and see much better results.

## Who's Who - Identifying your Target Networking Prospects

Power networking doesn't bring results if you're meeting just anyone. You need to identify key 'prospects' that can benefit you and find out where you have an opportunity to meet them. Who do you want to have in your network? You need to identify these individuals and go out and find them.

## Power Networking - What to Say and How to Say it

Once you know who you want to connect with, where to find them and have your book and services to offer, you need to know what you're going to say. To make power networking as effective as possible, you need to draft actual hypothetical conversations and practice them. This way, you're going to go into your interactions fully prepared.

## Power Networking Followup Strategies and Etiquette

The follow-up is crucial in power networking. You can meet a hundred people a day but nothing will ever happen if you don't follow up with them. This is how your initial meeting grows into a relationship, and that's what you should be aiming for.

## A Game Plan for your Power Networking

Nothing in life gets done without a good, solid game plan and the same goes for power networking. Even though you should always be in the networking mindset and meet people everywhere you go, you'll get the best results if you're organised and you have a clear plan to follow.

## Measuring your Networking Results

The only way to know whether your networking efforts are working or not, is to measure your results. You can't just assume that things are going well because you feel good. You need some kind of hard data that tells you whether or not your hard work is paying off. Measuring results is also a good motivator that keeps you focused by showing the progress you've made, for example book sales!

## Maintaining a Positive Mindset for Power Networking

In power networking, a positive mindset is absolutely essential. You need to be positive in order to motivate yourself to get out there and meet people. It's frightening to walk into a room full of strangers who all know each other but don't know you. If you radiate positivity, it attracts people to you.

To master the art of networking, please take a look at my workshop. Available at www. allthingswriting.com.au/online-training-programs

**Keynote Speaking Opportunities**

The most successful way to get your book and your business noticed and make more sales is by seeking out keynote speaking opportunities. The easiest way is to Google networking groups that would be interested in your topic. Make a list of these and contact them.
If you need any help around this, please contact me for further information at sue@allthingswriting.com.au.

## Build Your Community

## Blogging for your Business

Your blog is another form of social media...but one you have lots of control over!

## The Benefits of Blogging

A business blog is an asset to corporate bloggers and individual entrepreneurs alike. It's a source of low-cost, highly targeted leads, a showcase for your expertise, an opportunity to build relationships with your customers, and a magnet for traffic to your website. Wow!

Like social media, your blog lets you connect with your customers in a more personal way. It's interactive. It makes you a living human being instead of a static website. People can get to know your purpose, meaning, values, and ethics, which, in turn makes them like and trust you.

Your blog gives you a chance to demonstrate your expertise and establish your credibility. This is where you show your customers what you know with your posts. Since your posts change frequently, this will build your credibility.

Through your blog, you have the most cost-effective marketing at your fingertips. It combines low-cost marketing and promotion of your book or services with a way to get information on your target market through their comments and your stats.

If you have a website, writing as little as one post a week on your blog will increase your standing in the search engines. When you practice SEO (search engine optimisation) with your posts, you'll climb higher and faster in the rankings.

Successful blogging is a bit art and a bit science.

## 10 Excellent Blogging Tips

Some of these tips have been alluded to before, but they're so spot on they need to be mentioned in greater detail.

1. Be clear about what your readers are to do. Give clear calls to action in each blog post. Give clear action steps if needed, tell them to sign up for your newsletter, and explicitly ask them to share your posts.

2. Promote, promote, promote. Get the news out there in every way you can: optimise your blog, announce your posts, and connect with other bloggers.

3. Pay attention to your customers. Don't let your blog lay dormant, update it and make a commitment to it for the long term.

4.   Monitor your comments. It's a great connection with your customers. Comments make you seem friendly, and they build trust.

5.   Write suck-you-in headlines for your posts. Grab readers' attention and make them curious to learn more about what you have to say.

6.   Share your content every way you can and with everyone. You're giving away information for free because valuable free information will keep your readers coming back.

7.   Put buttons on your blog. Use every share button you can - Facebook "Like" buttons, Twitter and Pinterest buttons, etc.

8.   Use more than text. A great thing about blogging is that it's so easy to incorporate all sorts of videos, images, etc. Your readers will appreciate it and share them.

9.   Give comment love. Encourage your readers to comment and always reply.

10.  Remember - your blog is a business. Maintain it. Make a schedule to blog. Check comments and stats to know how you're doing.

Would you like to become a master at Blogging? Check out my workshop.

## Getting Noticed

When it comes to selling your book, nothing is more important than the quality of the book itself. If you have a good book, pitching it and attracting word-of-mouth advertising will be easy.

Sourcebottle is another great way to get noticed as a writer. It is a free online service that connects journalists with sources, those sources are you! Journalists post call outs on Sourcebottle for people to write articles on many different topics. Simply sign up and receive emails that will notify you of what topics are being sourced for stories.

However, when it comes to selling your book, the next most important thing is the quality of your sales pitch. Even if your book is excellent, you won't get a lot of word-of-mouth advertising unless at least a few brave souls are willing to purchase your book initially to kick things off. The only way that will happen is if you persuade them to. That's where copywriting comes in.

Copywriting, for the uninitiated, is the art of using sales copy to persuade readers to become buyers. Following are some guidelines to help you to craft compelling headlines for your blogs:

## Crafting a Winning Headline for your Blog

There are four important components of any winning headline. Let's take a look at them:

## 1. Speak to Your Audience

Your first job is to do some research about your industry. The purpose of this research is simple. In order to write a good blog, you need to speak directly to your readers, not to "readers in general." I mentioned this in the chapter around your target market. It means you must know something about your prospective buyers: their ages, their tastes and preferences, and their nationalities, for instance.

You will want to know where they come from, what they want, and most importantly, why your book would be a good solution to a problem or problems they have. Without having this information, your chances of writing a compelling blog are poor.

With this in mind, think hard before you start hammering out your first headline. Think about your target group, their desires, and the particular problem that your book solves. Make sure your message is succinctly and clearly in your headline.

## 2. Use Psychological Trigger Words

When it comes to writing a winning headline, few things are more important than psychological triggers. These are words that evoke a positive psychological response in your readers, independently of whatever is said about your book.

As an example, "free" is a psychological trigger word. So, if you're planning to give a product or service for free, include the actual word in your headline. It will catch visitors' eyes and lure them to read further.

Another powerful trigger word is "tested." For instance, you might say something like "This book contains dozens of tested and proven strategies that I have used for years." This will convey to the reader that your product isn't just any product; it is one that has been evaluated and tested by many trials over time.

Other powerful triggers include words like pioneering, surefire, crammed, soar, growth, explosive, secret, scientific, research, breakthrough, truth, unlimited, and special.

So, next time you write a headline or even fill in a headline template, remember to use some of these psychological trigger words, so you can be sure to draw the greatest possible emotional response from your readers.

## 3. Use a Good Headline Formula

It might sound average and dull, but it works. Start your headline with something like "Who Else Wants to Make $700 in the next 3 days?" or "Who Else Wants to Learn the Secrets of a Reclusive Millionaire?" or "Who Else Wants to Become Wealthy Beyond Your Wildest Dreams?" All of these different approaches will work; and they will work because you started with "Who Else Wants to..."

Alternatively, consider starting with something like "What Everyone Should Know About..." This will draw readers in by playing upon their lack of knowledge about what you are going to say. They will think "Well, I don't know that secret, so maybe I should read on."

When it comes to headline formulas, you have a lot of options. Pick a good one and put it to use.

## 4. State a Major Benefit or Propose a Puzzling Question

When writing headlines, your goal should always be to hook the reader. You don't have to provide useful information, (however it is highly recommended) tell them something new, or offer them the world. All you have to do is to give them a very, very good reason to keep reading. If they stick around to do that, they might just learn something about your book and could even buy it as a result.

So how can you do this? There are several ways as shown below:

1. State a benefit that your book provides that none others can. When it comes to drawing a reader in, few things work better than clearly differentiating your book from all others. If you do this successfully, your readers will have an "ah-ha" moment, where they realise why your book is so much better than the other options available. If you can get them to do this while they're reading the headline—rather than later—this is always good.

2. Suggest a benefit by issuing a brash order. Rather than asking a question or softly stating a benefit, forcefully order your reader to do something. For instance "Become a millionaire in just two years!" or "Live an extra 20 years by applying these 7 secrets of longevity." By commanding your readers to do something, rather than suggesting it, you will subconsciously push them to take action.

3. Propose a question. For instance, ask your readers what they would do if they suddenly became rich overnight. How would they spend that money? What

charities would they donate to? Use this as a way to make them think about how their lives will change after using the recommendations in your book. Then specifically say that your book will make it happen.

4. Frame your book's primary benefit as a newsworthy item. As mentioned earlier, an excellent way to hook people with your headline is to make it newsworthy. Consider writing it in the third person, talking about the newsworthy features of your book, and framing it as an important development in your niche. If your book is indeed innovative and good, then there's nothing wrong with using this method.

In short, use your headline to communicate at least one major benefit of your book; or to propose at least one thought-provoking question.

## Headline Templates

Let's take a look at some "fill-in-the-blanks" headlines. All you have to do is pick a headline from the correct category, fill in the blanks, and use it for your book title, sub-title or blog headings. Shape the rest of your content around your chosen headline.

## News-Style Headlines

1. Reclusive Internet Tycoon Finally Reveals Secret to Success in [Name of Niche] Niche

2. [Your Business] Launches Powerful New Product that Promises to Change the Market for [Product Niche]

3. After [# of Years] Years, [Product Niche] Will Finally Witness a Major Innovation

4. New Product Shakes Up Market for [Product Niche]

5. Age-Old Secret Helps People to Become More Successful in Their [Profession/Hobby]

6. Getting Rich Doesn't Always Have to be Hard, Says [Your Name]

7. Pioneer, [Your Business Name], Offers Solutions Where Other Businesses Cannot

8. Shocking Developments are on the Horizon, says Internet Mogul

9. [Your Business] Unveils Master Plan to Revolutionise the Market for [Product Niche]

10. Internet Mogul Claims that She Knows Why You'll Never Succeed at [Task/Hobby/Profession]

11. News Flash: This Innovative New Idea Might Just Change How You Do Business… for Good

Writing a good blog is never an easy task. And perhaps hardest of all is writing a good headline. Striking the right balance between enticing the reader with language and hooking them with a benefit or a question can often be very difficult. Fortunately for you, these guidelines take much of the hard work out of the process.

From here, you determine your own path. You might start by using the advice I've given for writing headlines. Craft a few of your own, think about how you would react to them, and ask a friend, neighbour, or colleague to evaluate the quality of your blog.

Once you have gotten the hang of writing headlines in general, think harder about your niche in particular. Do market research if needed; and think long and hard about how the average buyer thinks, and what that average buyer wants from a book like yours.

After you have answered these questions, grab a headline from one of the templates above; and then tailor it to your particular needs. Start by filling in the blanks, but if needed, go further and make alterations to the rest of the headline.

# Facebook

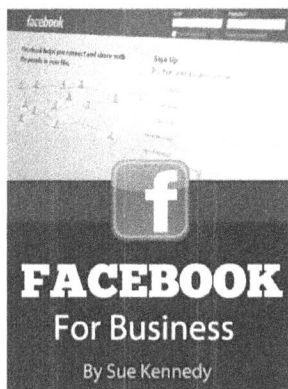

Is it worth using Facebook? The answer is "yes" and the reason is that today consumers have all the power, not the sales person! The true art of connecting with your audience is that of engagement. This is where social media has opened up the doors to doing business in a much easier way than ever before.

Following are some of the best practices with Facebook for Business:

- **Create engaging content** - your content should be a mix of different formats of content, like videos, images, events, polls and links to blogs or articles. Ask your audience questions!

- **Engage with your fans** - remember to completely focus on engagement. Ask questions, post helpful tips, and links to articles that your audience can 'like' and 'share'.

- **Facebook Groups** - a group on Facebook is a community of people with specific or common interests.

- **Don't oversell your products or services** - people don't like it if you are always selling to them, think about how you feel when others do it to you. Use the 80/20 rule for your sales messages versus your content posts. As an example, if you post five times a week, make one of those posts your sales message and the rest should be helpful or fun posts.

- **Create custom tabs** - these are like landing pages within your Facebook page, which you can use as calls to action to feature anything you like.

- **Add milestones** - use this feature to highlight some of your accomplishments like winning awards, product releases, major events, book launch, or any other accolades you can share.

- **Use Facebook insights** - this is facebook's internal analytics tool that helps you measure and analyse your Facebook presence. This is an amazing tool that gives you some very interesting and important information to help you with your content strategies.

- **Use hashtags** - these are a great way for you to share your promotions across multiple channels, increase the discoverability of your content, and centralise engagement with certain content, promotion, events, etc.

- **Use questions/polls for fan feedback** - in your status update section, you have the ability to post a question or a poll (click on 'add poll options'). This is a great way to ask your fans for feedback about your products/services or even the content you post to your timeline. The possibilities here are endless, and it's a great way to engage with your fans to increase the participation on your page.

## Pinterest

### Getting Started on Pinterest

Pinterest is one of the fastest-growing social media sites, quickly pushing ahead of the pack and making its way to number three behind Facebook and Twitter, and who knows where it will go from there. It used to be predominantly popular with young women, but now everyone uses it. Pinterest is a great way to promote your business online, no matter what you sell.

What makes Pinterest unique is its visual aspect. You create, organise, and manage your own boards with images that relate to your business. Although visual in nature, these "pins" can be videos, bits of text, infographics, or other things besides images. Any kind of content works, but it's the presentation of the content that makes the difference.

## What Pinterest can do for your Business

There are a number of ways Pinterest can help your business. First of all, it gets you traffic. It's not just friends and followers who will see your pinned content. Boards can appear in search engine results, giving the whole world access to your work.

Using Pinterest also has SEO benefits for your site. Similar to back links from Facebook and Twitter, back links from your Pinterest boards help raise your rank in the search engines.

If used correctly, Pinterest can be a highly effective lead-capturing tool. Visitors click the links on your profile or boards, which then direct them to your website where you can have an opt-in form for them to join your list. There aren't a whole lot of businesses doing this, so you can stand out in your niche.

Best of all, Pinterest helps you build your brand. Your profile communicates your brand message and your pins show what you're all about. It's not just about promoting and selling, but showing people what your business is all about.

## Optimise your Pinterest Profile

Your profile on Pinterest should be unique and interesting. It's what is going to attract people to your boards and to the content you have to offer. Your profile is also going to attract the search engines, so it needs to be optimised as thoroughly as possible for web searches.

## Keyword Optimising your Profile

Start by choosing several good keywords that have high search volume and relevance to your business. Use these keywords throughout your profile wherever you can, but keep it natural. Write profile content that explains to visitors what your business is about, but try to slip in your targeted keywords here and there.

Place your main keyword as close as possible to the beginning of your description. This is how your profile will be indexed by the search engines.

Your 'About' text is also very important. Although it should be short, try to include two or more targeted keywords. This field is the meta description that are commonly used on search engine result pages (SERPs) to display preview snippets for a given page, following is a couple of examples:

⬤Testimonials - - All Things Writing
allthingswriting.com.au/about-us/testimonials/ ▾
Thank you Sue Kennedy for your editing prowess. I am really thankful that you were recommended to me and that you were able to edit my first book.

⬤Set of 3 Books By Sue Kennedy - - About Sue
suekennedy.com.au/store/books/set-3-books/ ▾
Set of 3 books - Offline to online, The Power of LinkedIn, & Google Plus Training.

## Your Profile Content

In your profile content, try to describe your business in as few words as possible. Keep in mind that people may just be skimming the text. You want to impart what your company is all about, even if visitors just take a quick look. Prominently feature what's unique about your business.

Try to also include a call to action to get viewers to go to your website. Remember that your Pinterest profile is going to be driving traffic to your site. Tell people who visit your Pinterest profile what they will find when they click your link.

Be sure to fill out all of the profile fields completely.

Each field is an opportunity to get both readers and search engines interested in your business.

## Profile Optimisation Tips

Probably the most important part of your profile is your logo. Remember that Pinterest is a visually-oriented site. Choose your brand's logo or an image that's consistent with your brand's image. It should be clear to anyone who visits your Pinterest that it's your business's profile.

In your profile, link to your website, blog, and any other social media profiles you have. This helps your brand across platforms, letting visitors know that it's your business's profile they're looking at. Linking with other sites will also increase your traffic to each.

Finally, make sure that you're not hiding from the search engines. There is a 'hide' option in your Settings that's set as a default when you first sign up for Pinterest. Change this in your settings to "Off" before you go live.

## Don't wait for them to come to you

First and foremost, Pinterest is a social media site. This means that the connections you make with other users are going to be just as valuable, if not more valuable, than anything you to do optimise your profile. Once your profile is up and running, get out there and interact with other users.

## Embrace and Grow your Business

Social media is the next best thing to networking. Which platform should you use? It does really depend on your market and what business you are in. Where does your audience hang out? That is what you need to ask yourself before you commit to any social media platform. In most instances, LinkedIn is ideal, hence why I have included it in this book. I am going to talk about how LinkedIn Groups in particular can help promote you and your business.

Did you know that LinkedIn has more than 394 million users and more than 2 million Groups? These numbers should excite you tremendously due to the sheer size of the opportunity that it means for you and your business.

According to LinkedIn, the break down for users in its platform is 56% male and 44% female. The audience on LinkedIn is well educated, with half having a college degree and 44% earning more than 75K yearly. What's more, 84% of adults are on LinkedIn, according to Sprout Social. This is a huge opportunity for you, if you know what to do.

More than likely you already have a presence to some degree on LinkedIn. Perhaps you've optimised your profile and occasionally recommend someone or they recommend you. But are you getting the results you want? You may not be using LinkedIn as effectively as you can to attract new customers and grow your business.

In particular, the LinkedIn Groups feature offers an exceptional means of attracting new clients so that you can grow your business. However, most people don't know how to use LinkedIn Groups for maximum results.

Most people join Groups full of colleagues and associates, instead of potential clients. For example, if you're a graphic designer, you'll want to join groups to talk to other graphic designers. However, if you want to get more clients to expand your business, you need to join Groups that consist of your ideal audience.

That's just one small example of how you're likely using LinkedIn Groups in the wrong way. If you would like to know more on how you can maximise exposure to your target market with LinkedIn Groups, perhaps you would be interested in the workshop on LinkedIn for Groups. Available at www. allthingswriting.com.au/online-training-programs

**Expand your Network and Grow your Business**

According to research, LinkedIn is more effective than any other social media platform in generating leads and prospects. As for the Groups feature, there are a lot more benefits than you might realise.

**Create an Effective Profile**

Now that you understand the benefits of participating in, creating, and managing LinkedIn Groups, let's cover a few housekeeping points. Your profile is the most important part of your LinkedIn account. When people click through to view your profile, it should give them the type of information that will make them want to connect with you. You want your profile to look attractive so that you can spread the right message to your customers. This can only happen with a plan and the knowledge of what to do.

## Target the Most Beneficial LinkedIn Groups

Once you have created, updated, and optimised your profile, it's time to identify Groups that will help you increase your exposure and build relationships with target clients. It is important to understand which groups are the right ones for you and your business.

## Use Groups to Build Relationships

Now that you've identified Groups that you want to join, you need to know how to get active in them. It is important to learn how to craft a plan of action that will expand your reputation as a credible influencer in your Groups.

Remind yourself of the rules of each Group before you begin. You want to avoid dropping in to post promotions or auto-posting blogs to the ones you join. Over-promotion and automation will not provide the desired results. Instead, it may alienate you from the group.

## Build a Prosperous LinkedIn Group of your own

Managing your own LinkedIn Group is a very effective way of spreading brand awareness, building your authority, developing thought leadership, and so much more. Whatever your objectives are for your Group, you can achieve them if you give it some thought and make a cohesive plan of action.

## Common LinkedIn Mistakes to Avoid

As you move forward with using LinkedIn Groups to attract new customers and grow your business, there are a few common mistakes that people make on LinkedIn that you should avoid.

- **Not Having a Complete Profile** – Make sure your profile is as complete as possible. Don't be afraid of making initial mistakes, as you can always update your profile whenever you want. Take the time to fill out your profile with your audience in mind, so that they know you're the right person to connect with when they find you.
- **Not Having Links in your Profile** – If you don't include links to your website, you're missing out on a potentially huge traffic generator. In addition, anyone who wants to work with you will want to see your business website.
- **The Wrong Type of Graphics** – LinkedIn is a more conservative social media network. It is more professionally oriented than other social media networks, so make sure you're careful about the type of headshot you use, as well as other graphics you share. Use high quality, professional graphics directed toward your audience's sensibilities. This is not the place to post pictures of your dogs.
- **Being too much of a Salesperson** – Even though you have excellent information that can change lives, you must avoid being too sales focused.

Concentrate instead on building relationships before you start promoting a product or service.

- **Spreading Inaccurate Information** – Don't just share anything that comes across your feed, even if the message is from people you know and respect. Click through, check it out, and ensure that the information is accurate before sharing.
- **Updating your Status Infrequently** – Just like your email newsletter, don't wait too long between posts to your profile and your Groups. People will forget you exist and ignore your updates. Instead, choose a time of day best for your audience and post a status at that time every day.
- **Over-Posting Status Updates** – On Facebook and Twitter, the expectation is that updates occur frequently. Multiple times a day is often the norm. With LinkedIn, you don't want to over share. Most people believe that a status update more than once a day is too much on LinkedIn.
- **Sending Direct Spam** – Don't use LinkedIn to send direct messages to people without having engaged with them in some way in a group or elsewhere. Even if your information is important, people will view it as spam.
- **Being Negative in Posts** – Coming off as a know-it-all on any social media is a big no-no. Doing it on LinkedIn can ruin your intentions to spread awareness of your expertise and actually tarnish your reputation.
- **Not Differentiating your LinkedIn from Other Social Media** – Many people get on LinkedIn and treat it just like other social media platforms. It is

not the same and should be treated in a more business-like manner. Everything you put on LinkedIn should be focused on business.

- **Not Personalising Messages** – While tempting, using automatic systems to post to every social media account is not a good idea. Doing it on LinkedIn is definitely not advised. Ensure that each message you post, whether you are sharing an article or an image, is personalised.

**Create your Action Plan**

Now that you know the benefits of using LinkedIn and LinkedIn Groups to build your network and grow your business, you need to create a plan of action.

Remember, using LinkedIn Groups isn't about you. It's very tempting to make a profile for any social media all about you. If you do that, you won't get all of the benefits that social media offers. When you're using social media for business purposes, everything about your LinkedIn participation has to be about your audience and the objectives you've set for yourself.

Would you like to learn how to be more effective with LinkedIn Groups? Available at www. allthingswriting.com.au/online-training-programs

# Chapter Twelve

# Finishing Touches

*"We all need tools to help us on our journey"*

**Following are some resources to help you with completing your masterpiece:**

## Idea Tools

http://thinkbuzan.com/

https://mindnode.com/

https://www.xmind.net/

http://freemind.en.softonic.com/

https://www.mindmeister.com/

## Writing Tools

https://www.literatureandlatte.com/trial.php

https://www.amazon.com

http://www.sourcebottle.com

## Book Creation Tools

https://www.createspace.com/

## ISBN (International Standard Book Number)

http://www.myidentifiers.com

## Images

http://www.photodune.net

http://www.dreamstime.com

http://www.istockphoto.com

http://www.gettyimages.com.au

http://www.fotolia.com

http://www.shutterstock.com

http://www.bigstockphoto.com

## Quotes

http://www.brainyquote.com/

https://www.goodreads.com/quotes

http://www.keepinspiring.me/positive-inspirational-life-quotes/

http://www.inc.com/lolly-daskal/100-motivational-quotes-that-will-inspire-you-to-succeed.html

http://www.entrepreneur.com/article/247213

http://addicted2success.com/quotes/30-famous-quotes-that-will-inspire-success-in-you/

I know I said this earlier, but I want to say it again…

**Congratulations! You have completed your book, you should be very proud of yourself.** I would love to know how you went and how you are feeling. Please share your success with the world and me!

Love, gratitude and success to you always,

Sue

*All Things Writing*
——— SUE KENNEDY ———

## BONUS Chapter

## Writing Tips & Tricks

*"Your writing needs to be error free"*

## Top 10 Grammar and Punctuation Mistakes

Grammar and punctuation mistakes can make your writing seem uneducated and careless, but correcting those mistakes is not that difficult if you keep the following rules in mind.

It might not be a surprise to you that comma errors are at the top of the "Mistakes" list (along with misuse of "tricky" words).

## 1. Commas separating independent clauses

When two independent clauses are joined by a coordinating conjunction (and, or, nor, for, so, yet, but), you need a comma:

Sally went to school, and her father went to work. Jesse didn't feel well, so he stayed home.

## 2. Commas separating dependent and independent clauses

When a dependent clause precedes an independent clause, you need a comma:

If I leave work early today, I can get to the matinee.

When a dependent clause comes after an independent clause, you don't need a comma:

I can get to the matinee if I leave work early today.

## 3. Commas separating introductory words or phrases

An introductory phrase or group of words needs a comma unless it's very short.

On second thought, let's get pizza. Tonight we'll order pizza.

## 4. Sentence fragments

Every complete sentence requires a subject and a verb. Sentence fragments lack one or the other.

Home on the range. (no verb)
Ate some chicken for lunch. (no subject)

## 5. Verb-subject agreement

Subjects and verbs must agree in person and number. This can be confusing when the subject and verb are separated by a group of words:

Kylie, the girl in the orange dress and sneakers, is a junior.
People who are intelligent often enjoy playing chess.

## 6. Colons and semi-colons

Colons introduce lists or specific definitions:

Please buy these things at the store: matches, light bulbs, and cottage cheese.

Semi-colons separate clauses that are closely related:

We take the same classes in school; we both love biology.

## 7. Repeated subjects or objects

Other languages allow a subject or object to be repeated in its own clause, but English doesn't allow this. In other languages, this is correct:

The purse that had been stolen it was found. In English the correct sentence must be:

The purse that had been stolen was found. The same is true for objects:
Incorrect:

The little dog chased the car that his owner was riding in it.

Correct:

The little dog chased the car that his owner was riding in.

## 8. Parallelism

Items in a series should be the same. When you're using nouns, verbs, adjectives, etc. in a series, they should all agree.

Incorrect:

Sam loves skiing, running track, and basketball.

Correct:

Sam loves skiing, running track, and playing basketball.

## 9. Apostrophes

Many nouns and pronouns add 's' to form plurals, the 's is to show possession. It versus It's is a very good example since lots of people make a mistake with this pronoun.

It's means It is - It is a beautiful day.

Its means ownership - The computer was left on the bus by its owner.

## 10. Quotation Marks

Quotation marks indicate direct quotations or exact statements of others. Indirect statements, or making reference to what someone said doesn't require quotation marks.

Mum told Dad, "Please come home early from work tonight."
Mum asked Dad if he would please come home early from work tonight.

## Top 10 Tricky Words

Some words in the English language cause more problems than others. These ten sets of words are at the top of the list of troublesome words, but there are plenty more. The best thing to do if you are at all unsure is to look the word up.

### 1. Among/Between

Among is used with three entities

Between is used with two entities

The lottery was divided among several winners. Choose between waffles and pancakes.

### 2. Bad/Badly

Bad is an adjective describing a noun

Badly is an adverb

The boy was bad.
The boy was badly hurt by the fly ball.

### 3. Bring/Take

Bring means an object is being carried toward you.

Take means an object is being carried away from you.

Please bring me that book.
Please take these files to your desk.

## 4. Choose/Chose

Choose is a verb meaning "select."
Chose is the past tense of choose, meaning "selected."

Susan chose an ivory dress for her wedding.

You should choose the option that works best for you.

## 5. Fewer/Less

Fewer refers to items that can be counted

Less refers to uncountable amounts

Fewer people are in the middle class today.

Less sugar would make this a healthier drink.

## 6. Good/Well

Good is an adjective

Well is an adverb

She's a good girl.
She is feeling well today after being sick for a long time.

## 7. Loose/Lose

Loose is an adjective meaning "not tight."
Lose is a verb meaning either "to misplace" or "not to win."

Did you lose the dog, or did he get loose from his leash?

## 8. Their/There/They're

Their is a possessive adjective meaning "belonging to them."

There is an adverb referring to a location of something or someone.
They're is a shortened form of they are.

They're in the waiting room to pick up their children. You can find them there.

## 9. Two/To/Too

Two is a number

To is a preposition

Too is an adverb

You two boys are going to the cafeteria for breaks too many times.

## 10. Whose/Who's

Whose is a possessive pronoun.

Who's is a contraction of who is.

Whose hat is this? Who's going home now?

# Online Writing Tips

## Facebook

Do you know anyone who's not on Facebook? Probably not very many people, anyway. The biggest companies and the most successful business people all over the world are on Facebook. Why?

Because they see it's tremendous power - 24/7 - to build relationships with millions of people anywhere in the world...and on autopilot. That's the potential for making lots and lots of money, given the right formula.

## Facebook Tips that Work

Messages you leave on Facebook can increase your success or detract from it. These tips should help.

Develop your style - Keep your writing style in messages appropriate to Facebook. That means, informal and social, personal and appropriate. No heavy negativity or heavy sales pitch, either. You might want to write similar to the way you speak.

Keep it short and focused on the main point - Respect other people's time and stay on message. Give valuable information of interest - Giving people something they want or need by way of information is a way to start building a relationship.

When it comes to Facebook fan pages (where you post your products), these tips on posts might come in handy.

Write posts relevant to the topic of the fan page. Post questions and start discussions relevant to your target audience to encourage responses.

Analyse your posts. Look at the responses and likes you're getting. Are you missing the mark? Do your readers want something you're not providing? Pinpointing these issues will pay off in the future.

### Five things never to do on Facebook

1. Never spam. You want to promote and engage equally. No one wants to see posts full of links.

2. Keep your personal and professional pages separate. Combining them can confuse the reader and cause mistrust.

3. Never attack people. You won't please everyone. Just ignore the criticism and move past it. Or delete it.

4. Don't leave your fans stranded. The main point of social media is interaction. It makes you human.

5. Have a plan. What do you want to accomplish? If you don't know, you won't accomplish it.

## LinkedIn

LinkedIn has a big problem -- that's good! Most people still think of LinkedIn as ineffective for producing results in marketing. But the problem is not with LinkedIn; the problem is with the way people are approaching it.

As you probably know, LinkedIn is the largest professional network in the world. It's a place where professionals connect with each other and build a network of solid long-term relationships. These relationships can result in enormous sales of products and services, eventually. But it's all in your presenting approach.

## Tips for Presenting Yourself on LinkedIn

How you present yourself is very important on LinkedIn. It takes pride in distinguishing itself as a business site, so the informal atmosphere and approach encountered on Facebook or a blog is unacceptable.

## Profile

Your first chance to put your best face forward is on your profile. Your profile speaks for you. It's your first impression.

## Photo

Have a professional looking photo. No party hats here. You want people to use your services or buy your products, so look your best.

## Your URL

LinkedIn assigns you a non-descript URL by default. Edit this to use your own name if it's available. That way, people will find you more easily.

## Professional Headline

The keywords you want to be associated with should be in your headline. Searches are done on LinkedIn by scanning the keywords in each profile headline.

## Accurate, Engaging Summary

Your summary captures your entire career in a few words. Make it stand out by answering prospective clients' needs. Use keywords here as well.

## Accomplishments

Be accurate and specific about your accomplishments. Be relevant and quantify your accomplishments if possible.

Make your profile as interesting as possible. In your

case you are probably not applying for a job, so let people know who you are, what area(s) you work in, what products or services you offer, and what things make you stand out.

When you've completed your profile, don't walk away and hope for the best. There's an important protocol to follow to make yourself known in LinkedIn. You need to be assertive in order to be found, but in the way LinkedIn defines, which is different from anywhere else.

Using groups - As mentioned earlier, Groups can be of help to you in three ways: they can help develop your profile, assist with lead generation, and aid in your own professional development.

Promoting your events - Promotion is easy in LinkedIn once you have established yourself because the right groups are easily targeted with the result that your information can be quickly spread and your brand recognition will spread.

Using status updates - Status updates are underused in LinkedIn. Update your profile with relevant blog posts and other news items.

If you follow LinkedIn's guidelines, there's enormous potential for success.

## Twitter

Twitter is an outrageously successful social media platform that you no doubt already are somewhat familiar with. Basically, you have up to 140 characters per tweet to announce anything you want to.

Your general goals with Twitter are to generate as large a following as possible, to retain those followers, and to engage them so that they buy your products and services. If you're really good, your followers might retweet your message (send it to their Twitter friends) or even be "favourited," which will make you very popular.

So, the question is, "What do you have to do to create messages in 140 characters that are so intriguing that your followers and potential customers will click your link?"

## Tips for Great Tweets

Your tweets must interest the person reading them; that means they must be personal and be about things that interest the reader. Furthermore, what you really want is not just for the reader to click on your link, but also to share, like, recommend, tweet and forward your information and link. To accomplish this, you need to ask yourself some questions.

**What do you want your tweets to say about you and your brand? How can you make this "statement" appealing to the people following you?**

You need a sound knowledge of the value of your information, your brand, and your product or service. Your tweets act as spurts of information that capture the reader's attention and imagination.

**What appeals to your readers? What content are they looking for?**

Once you know this, you can begin to determine what information they want to get and how they want it presented. You can decide what to include in the recommendations, requests, questions, answers, invitations, and offers you send to them.

Try some of these tips:

1. Engage your audience emotionally by asking a question or suggesting that they do something.

2. Respond to every tweet you receive; you never know where it might lead.

3. Provide valuable, relevant information to your base. Credit the source if there is one.

4. Be truthful. Don't lie in order to get people to click on your link. You'll pay for it later.

5. Be brief. Keep your tweet focused on one point.

6. Don't "flood" your base with tweets. Be considerate and space out your tweets.

One way to think of your tweet is as if it were a headline. Create a question of some kind in the reader's mind so that they want to click the link to get more information. Be sure to leave a link. Use interesting terms or pop culture items or breaking news your readers can relate to. Choose something that will grab them and keep them.

## Tips on The Process of Review and Revision of your Book

After you finish the rough draft of your book, you should walk away from it for a bit of time. You've likely immersed yourself in mind-mapping the outline and transforming that into a rough draft with notes, reminders and thoughts you want to incorporate.

Stepping back for a while will give you a fresh new perspective on what you've accomplished so far and make the revision process much easier. It's up to you how long you wait before tackling review and revision.

For some, a few hours are enough and for others, it could take a day, week or even a month.

Proofreading is one of the easiest tasks when it comes to writing; however, it is one of the most essential steps to ensure you look like a professional.

Here are some ideas that you'll want to incorporate in the various stages of the revision process:

- Read from a hard copy in the beginning. Most professional writers find that errors or problems tend to be seen on paper more clearly than the computer screen.

- Read the rough draft straight through. Don't begin making corrections until you've read the entire book through to refresh your memory about the big issues that you want the book to address.

- Focus on the big picture at first. Forget about the commas and spelling during the first few runs through the draft. Right now, focus on whether your book addresses the questions and viewpoints you want your reader to come away with.
- Spell and grammar checking. These days we tend to write on our computers and use programs that have spell check and grammar check installed within them. It is very important that you use these

programs, however, keep in mind that they are not 100% accurate, they will not pick up everything. An example of this could be "they will meat later" should of course read "they will meet later". This is why it is important to go over your work more than once.

- Run-ons and fragments. Run-on sentences and sentence fragments are two of the most common errors for new writers. Please make sure that each clause is dependent and can stand alone. Make sure that you don't combine two unrelated clauses into one sentence.

- Misspelling confusing words. It is so easy to read right past words that are spelled correctly however, are actually the wrong words when you proofread. Make sure you look out for these, the most common problem words are: your/you're, they're/their, affect/effect, advise/advice, lie/lay, and sit/sat.

- Punctuation and capitalisation errors. These errors can also be easily missed when you don't proofread carefully. Please remember that every sentence begins with a capital letter and every sentence ends with a period or other end mark. Remember to check for comma errors and correct use of apostrophes.

- Make the prose flow. Are there areas of the book where your thoughts wander or you're confused? If you're experiencing that, your reader will also. Be sure your text flows seamlessly throughout the book.

- Does your book deliver what it promises? The purchaser and reader of your book had a reason for choosing it over the other offerings. Perhaps it was a blurb on the front or back cover that promised information about a subject or process that interested them. Be sure your book covers what you claim it will.

- Are your facts accurate? Check and recheck the facts that you present in the book to ensure their accuracy. Nothing can ruin your book for the reader than inaccuracy in the content.

- Does the book end properly? Your conclusion should tie everything in the book together and leave the reader happy that he or she bought and read what you had to say.

- Does it make sense? Finally, your book should make complete sense to the audience you're targeting. At this point, you may want to have another person who knows something of what you're writing about to look over the book and ask questions or comment.

You may go through several draft processes before you announce that your book is ready for a final review and edit. Some writers claim they can write a book in only one draft, but for most of us, it takes several.

## Conclusion

To sum up, have a good time with writing content in all its forms. Let your personality shine through readers like that and connect with it. Make it a conversation that speaks to your readers as if they are friends you care about.

At the same time, remember to give value by taking the time to make your content unique in some way. Show your readers that you respect them by making your writing correct.

If you don't remember the rules for punctuation, grammar, and word usage, brushes up on them.

Having a plan for what you want to say. Don't ramble or repeat yourself. It bores your readers and disrespects their time.

Present your ideas clearly. Simplicity is better than complexity, even when you're presenting complex ideas.

Finally, remember that you are writing for your business. Your ultimate goal is to make money. Relate your writing to products of value that turn your readers into buyers.

## BONUS Chapter

## Writing Templates

*"A professional writer makes life easier for themselves with planning and templates"*

# Your Writing Plan

## Name

_____

## My book is (fiction/non-fiction)_____

**The working title is**

_____

_____

**I plan to write (words/time per day)**_____

_____

**I plan to have my book finished by**_____

_____

**The goal for this book after I finish it is to**_____

_____

_____

_____

_____

_____

_____

_____

_____

_____

_____ **Signature & Date**

# Non-Fiction Writing Checklist

❑　Print, complete and sign your writing commitment plan.

❑　Set up a designated writing space.

❑　Make sure you have plenty of paper, pens, notebooks, etc.

❑　Print out the non-fiction worksheet pages.

❑　Choose your main topic.

❑　Choose a working title/subtitle.

❑　Write an outline.

❑　Use reliable research to gather more information.

❑　Write your content from your outline and notes.

❑　Proofread and edit your book.

❑　Decide what front matter and back matter you need for your book.

❑　Design your front and back cover.

❑　Use the worksheets to lay out all of the elements of your book.

❑　Format your book for your preferred publishing platform.

❑　Publish!

# Outline Worksheet

## 1. Identify your main topic
## 2. Identify your main categories (these will be your chapters)
## 3. Identify your sub-topics (should have a minimum of 2-4 per chapter)

## MAIN TOPIC

_____

## Category

_____

## Sub-topics (and if necessary, sub-subcategories)

_____

_____

_____

_____

## Category

_____

## Sub-topics (and if necessary, sub-subcategories)

_____

_____

_____

_____

## Category

_____

## Sub-topics (and if necessary, sub-subcategories)

_____

_____

_____

_____

# Category

---

# Sub-topics (and if necessary, sub-subcategories)

---

---

---

---

# Category

---

# Sub-topics (and if necessary, sub-sub-topics)

---

---

---

---

# Category

_____

# Sub-topics (and if necessary, sub-topics)

_____

_____

_____

_____

# Category

_____

# Sub-topics (and if necessary, sub-topics)

_____

_____

_____

_____

## Category

_____

## Sub-topics (and if necessary, sub-sub-topics)

_____

_____

_____

_____

## Category

_____

## Sub-topics (and if necessary, sub-sub-topics)

_____

_____

_____

_____

## Category

_____

## Sub-topics (and if necessary, sub-sub-topics)

_____

_____

_____

_____

## Category

_____

## Sub-topics (and if necessary, sub-sub-topics)

_____

_____

_____

_____

# Category

_____

# Sub-topics (and if necessary, sub-sub-topics)

_____

_____

_____

_____

# Category

_____

# Sub-topics (and if necessary, sub-sub-topics)

_____

_____

_____

_____

## Category

_____

## Sub-topics (and if necessary, sub-sub-topics)

_____

_____

_____

_____

## Category

_____

## Sub-topics (and if necessary, sub-sub-topics)

_____

_____

_____

_____

## Category

---

## Sub-topics (and if necessary, sub-sub-topics)

---

---

---

---

# Mind map Worksheet

If you prefer mind mapping to outlining, here is an example you can use. You can of course free-form your own, or use mind mapping software.

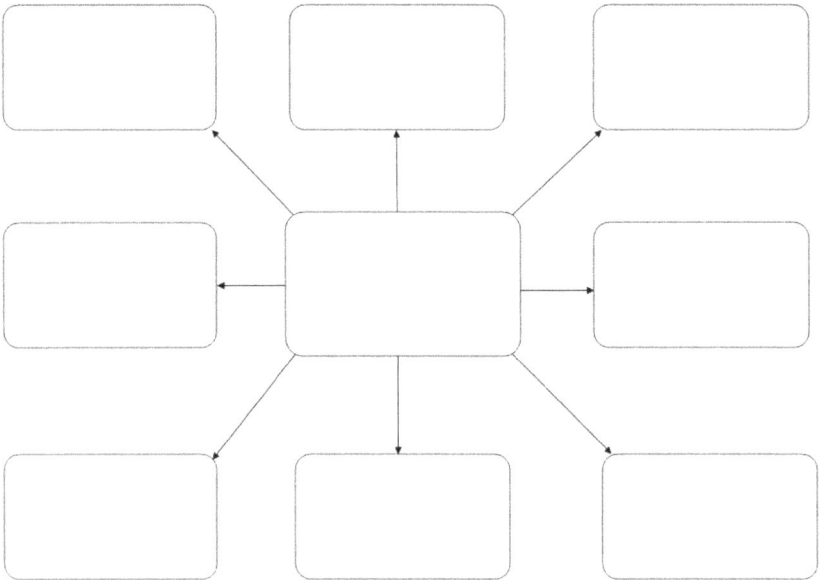

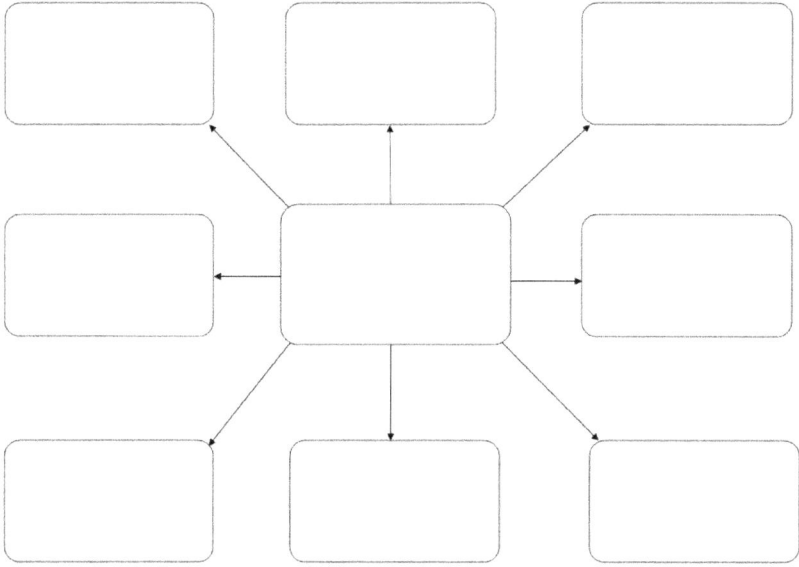

# Front Book Cover

Use this page to lay out your idea for a book cover. Think about title, subtitle, and author name placement, any images you want to include, etc.

# Back Book Cover

Design the back cover for your book. Brief description, author bio, bullet points, etc.

# Book Title Page

Title: Subtitle: Author: Website: Publisher:

# Front Matter Page

*Title Page ~ Copyright ~ Dedication ~ Table of Contents ~ Acknowledgments ~ Preface ~ Foreword*

# Back Matter Page

*Afterword ~ Coming Soon ~ Appendix ~ About the Author ~ Other Call to Action (eg. Other books)*

# Fiction Writing Checklist

❑    Print, complete and sign your writing commitment plan.

❑    Set up a designated writing space.

❑    Make sure you have plenty of paper, pens, notebooks, etc.

❑    Print out the fiction worksheet pages.

❑    Decide the type of fiction and the length you'll write.

❑    Choose a working title.

❑    Introduce yourself to your story's characters.

❑    Write a story synopsis using the story map.

❑    Use a story board to further discover your story's plot and subplots.

❑    Write your book from your worksheets/storyboards.

❑    Proofread and edit your book.

❑    Decide what front matter and back matter you need for your book.

❑    Design your front and back cover.

❑    Use the worksheets to lay out all of the elements of your book.

❑    Format your book for your preferred publishing platform.

❑    Publish!

# Title Ideas Page

You have a working title, but maybe it's not working hard enough? List other title possibilities as they come to you, then come back and review them with fresh eyes later.

_____

_____

_____

_____

_____

_____

_____

# Character Worksheet

Use this sheet to plan and get an understanding of your characters.

**You may need to print additional character pages.**

Character Name and Physical Description:

What does he/she need and want?

What is at stake for the character?

What change will the character experience?

Character Name and Physical Description:

What does he/she need and want?

What is at stake for the character?

What change will the character experience?

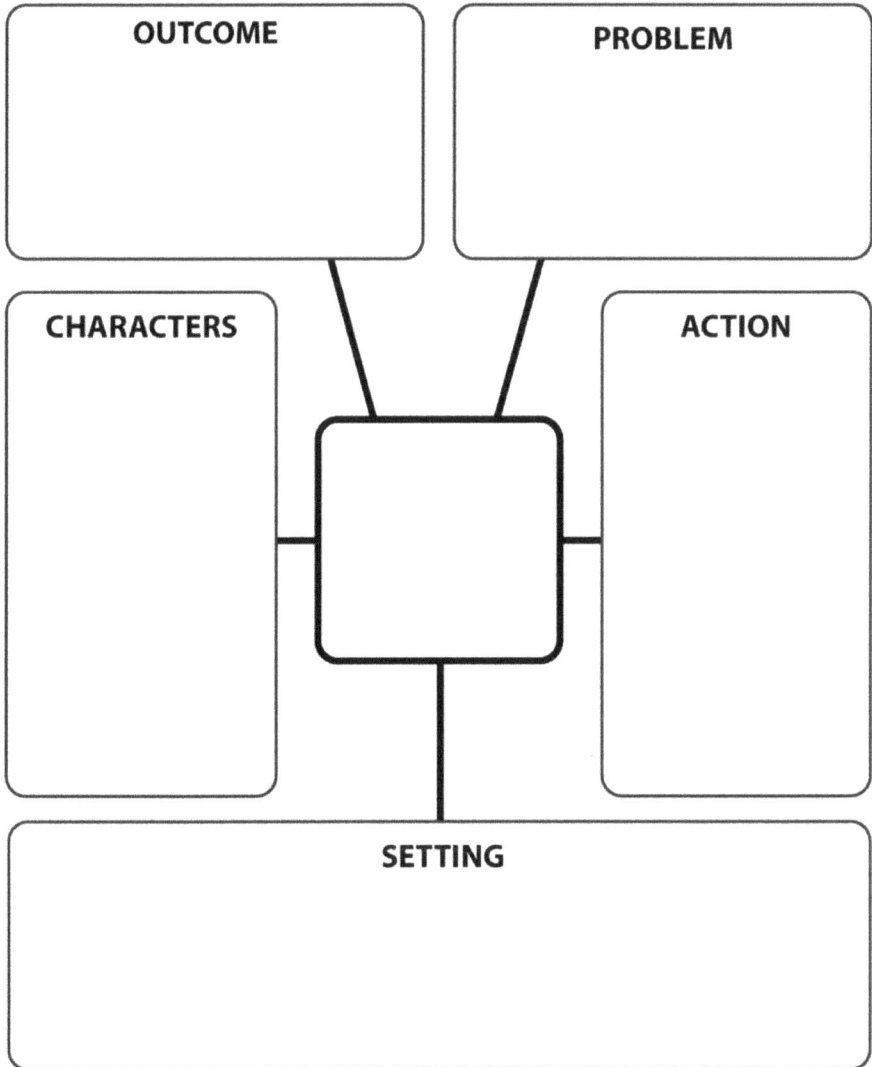

# Story Map

OUTCOME

PROBLEM

CHARACTERS

ACTION

SETTING

Use the story map to create your story synopsis. This is a summary of what happens in your story.

# Story Board

# About the Author

Words have the power to change the world!

Sue Kennedy founded her company on the core belief that everyone has a book in them.

Sue believes in the philosophy that every time you communicate, you have an opportunity to impact and influence people's lives.

With her signature programs, Sue provides her clients with strategic, creative and surprisingly fun techniques to express their hidden genius and tap into the full extent of who they are and what they can become.

As an International Strategic Writing Coach for elite experts, entrepreneurs and Best Selling Authors to C-suite executives, Sue has helped thousands of individuals take an ordinary communication opportunity and turn it into a memorable experience — one marked by authenticity, originality, creativity, confidence, impact and lasting results.

For over 20 years, Sue's Elite Writing Mastery Series has given writers a learning experience, which transforms their teams.

Sue hosts her annual writers retreats: a 3-day experience for aspiring writers, entrepreneurs and executives who want to become world class, best selling, award winning authors where they all come together to meet, connect, brainstorm, create and bring their ideas into the world.

Sue is widely regarded as one of Australia's leading strategic thinkers, business speakers and educators in the field of business writing.

She is the founder and Managing Director of All Things Writing, a consultancy firm offering training, coaching, mentoring, facilitation, and keynote speaking services to clients across a wide range of industries since 2005.

Not only is Sue an outstanding strategic thinker and facilitator, she is also an entertaining presenter. She has presented keynote presentations and workshops for executives to thousands of companies, from industries as diverse as pharmaceutical, utility, retail, security, FMCG, financial services, logistics and transport, professional services and many others.

As a facilitator, she has helped organisations develop and implement their business writing training and development strategy. Client industries include, pharmaceutical, media, health industry, security, financial services, and retail, amongst others. She has worked as a facilitator for BNI (Business Networking International), Nepean Community College, BEC (Business Enterprise Centre), Parramatta Community College, amongst others.

**Sue Kennedy signature keynotes include:**
- The Author Within – business writing excellence
- Business writing email excellence
- Rockin Content Creation
- From boring to WOW newsletters
- Killer Headlines that get noticed
- Discover the magic of mind mapping
- The power of business blogging – discover the 10 secrets of how you are losing thousands of dollars
- How to get instant authority through your writing
- Discover the art of story telling
- Taking business writing to the customer experience
- Copywriting (101) for entrepreneurs
- Copywriting for business
- Copywriting for professional writers
- Writing for public speaking
- Writing for presentations
- Writing tips and tricks

Sue Kennedy is available as a Keynote Speaker, or as

a Trainer, and Coach. Sue has written for various types of media and has presented and trained on many topics:

**Business & Marketing**

- Social Media Management
- Mobile Marketing for Business
- Simple Podcasting Secrets
- Pinterest for Business
- The Power of List Building
- Video Marketing for Beginners
- Powerpoint Tips and Tricks
- Target Marketing
- Content Branding
- Evernote
- Visual Content Marketing
- Marketing Plan
- Business SEO
- Mailchimp
- Facebook for Business
- Website Optimisation
- Instagram for Business
- Effective Emails
- Plus many more…

**To request Sue as a speaker, please email for booking availability at:**

sue@allthingswriting.com.au

# Next Steps

# A Hero's Journey

**Everyone has a book inside of them, but it doesn't do any good until you get it out**
**Give someone the greatest gift of all time**
**Their life story in a book**

A Hero's Journey Publishers will write the story of your loved one as a gift.

Their life story created in book form. These books will become heirlooms for the family.

The service includes:

- We interview the loved one anywhere in the World.
- We transcribe the interview to ensure we capture their unique voice.
- We then professionally ghost write the story, so it is great and easy to read.
- We professionally edit the book.

- We professionally proof the book.
- We professionally design the book cover with a graphic artist.
- We print one copy for the gift giver to approve.
- We print the final gift copy with various finishes available to choose from. For example leather bound, hardcopy, paperback.
- You can then choose to print one only or as many as you need for the family to have in their collection as a keepsake.
- The family member who's story it belongs to, could then sign each copy with a special message.
- Everything is done from the beginning to the end.
- The ultimate gift is ideal for adult children to give as a gift to their aging parents. For example at their 50th Wedding Anniversary.

**Our Mission**:

Everyone has a book inside of them, but it doesn't do any good until you get it out. Our mission is to get it out and into a book for the family to have as an heirloom.

For more information on how we can make this journey a reality, please email sue@allthingswriting.com.au

Please like us on Facebook!
(www.facebook.com/aherosjourney)

# A Professional Journey

# The Author Within Writer's Retreat Prospectus

**Unique Features**

- Success metrics for book writing excellence

- Practical and pragmatic insights for book writing

- Easy to use tips and tools

- Hands-on application

- Highly engaging and fully interactive

- 12 month coaching and mentoring program

## Benefits of Attending

- Learn how to focus before you write your first word

- Understand the "Why" behind writing your book

- Surround yourself with experts and like minded people

- Ooze a multitude of inspiration with your retreat surroundings

- Receive a tremendous amount of constructive feedback

- Gain all the confidence you need to succeed in writing your book

- Receive all the assistance, planning, design, marketing, PR, plus many tips and tricks to help with your writing

## Who Should Attend

- Small business owners who want to be the authority in their market

- People that want to have credibility in their market

- Small business owners that strive to be the best in their market. Those that wish to be successful leaders in their field of excellence

# Writer's Retreat Outline

## Day One

### Session 1:

Discover how writers are born from nothing

- Individual practical exercise
- Learn how to think on your feet
- Learn how to face your fears
- Learn how articulate you are
- Uncover your storytelling abilities
- Learn the art of vulnerability
- Learn how to unveil yourself creatively

### Session 2:

Uncover the writer within you

- Individual practical exercise
- Brainstorming creativity session to answer the initial critical questions you have as a writer to be
- Discover your passion as a writer
- Understand what you would like to write about

**Session 3:**

Learn the 2 absolute secrets to writing success

- Individual practical exercise and discussions
- Determine why there are 2 types of people and what they are
- Meditation: "Discover how you structure time inside yourself"

**Session 4:**

Learn how to express your thoughts

- Individual practical exercise
- Brainstorm what your book will be about
- Understand what makes a compelling story
- Understand the different types of storytelling

**Session 5:**

Unveil your unique reader

- Interactive exercise
- Understand your audience
- Discover who you are writing for
- Create a profile of your reader that helps you write just for them

**Day Two**

**Session 6:**

Uncover your style as a writer

- Individual practical exercise, and discussions

- Understand your style as a writer

- Understand your readers style to ensure you speak their language

- Uncover the 4 tones to choose from as a writer

- Understand the 4 ways your reader processes inside their mind

- Discover the 3 languages of your readers unconscious mind

- Learn your own language and avoid the common pitfalls of authors who only know how to speak their own language and eliminating 2/3 of their readers

**Session 7:**

Learn the psychology behind how to write

- Individual practical exercise, and discussions

- Uncover the quick and easy way to write your book effectively and efficiently so that you avoid it taking a lifetime

- Learn the basic structure of book development in 15 minutes

## Session 8:

Discover the secret resources of writers

- Listening and learning session

- Powerful tools to create your book

- Discover the pros and cons of different tools

- Learn the boring bits that are necessary including the legal stuff!

- Receive a step-by-step guide of resources

## Session 9:

Uncover the importance of research writers do before they put pen to paper

- Interactive exercise

- Discover what words work best

- Understand the importance of your book cover

- Research and understand what your cover should look like

- Create your book cover brief for your designer

## Session 10:

Discover the importance of everyday inspiration

- Interactive exercise
- Discover what inspires you
- Brainstorm all types of inspirations
- Learn the 20 secrets of inspiration
- Learn the importance of creating a special writer's nook
- Create you writer's nook inside your environment
- Learn the 10 secrets to high productivity as a writer
- Learn where to find images for your book

## Session 11:

Special Ritual for Writer's

- Interactive exercise
- Discover what type of writer you are
- Learn what the different archetypes are for writers

## Day Three

## Session 12:

Learn how to put your first draft down

- Interactive exercise

- Identify what the 10 steps are for your first draft
- Putting pen to paper!

## Session 13:

Uncover the 16 secrets to marketing success

- Listening and learning session
- The importance of your front cover
- The importance of your back cover
- What your BIO and picture should look like
- The importance of the 'other' internal pages of your book

## Session 14:

Tips & Tricks of proofreading & editing to polish your work

- Listening and learning session
- Understand the importance of proofreading
- Understand the importance of editing
- Understand the importance of formatting

## Session 15:

Taking your baby to market

- Listening and learning session

- Learn how to finalise your book

- Discover how to become a Number 1 Best Seller – this normally costs $3000, however, it is free to you

- Detailed administration steps of what you will be required to do like EIN, ISBN etc

## Session 16:

Uncover your writing for maximum engagement

- Listening and learning session

- Learn how to create your tribe

- Identify where your market is

- Discover and understand why you need social media

- Overview on the importance of Blogging, speaking events, LinkedIn groups, and networking

- BONUS 1 Writing Tips & Tricks

- BONUS 2 Templates

## Session 17:

Looking back over the last 3 days

- Interactive exercise

- Determine where you are now

- Determine how you move forward

**Session18:**

Wrap up & Gratitude of Thanks

- Interactive exercise

- Discover who is in the room

- Learning to give and receive

**To see if you qualify for our writer's retreat please email us**

**For a Free 15 minute strategy session at:**
sue@allthingswriting.com.au

*All Things Writing*
——— SUE KENNEDY ———

# Bulk Orders.

This book by Sue Kennedy is available at special quantity discounts for bulk purchases that can be used for marketing, promotions, fundraisers and/or educational purposes.

You could also use the book as a give away gift when clients purchase off you.

The book is very popular with corporate clients to give to their staff as a learning tool or as a thank you.

Contact sue@allthingswriting.com.au to discuss how we can accommodate your needs.

*All Things Writing*
—— SUE KENNEDY ——

# Other Books

# An Executive Journey

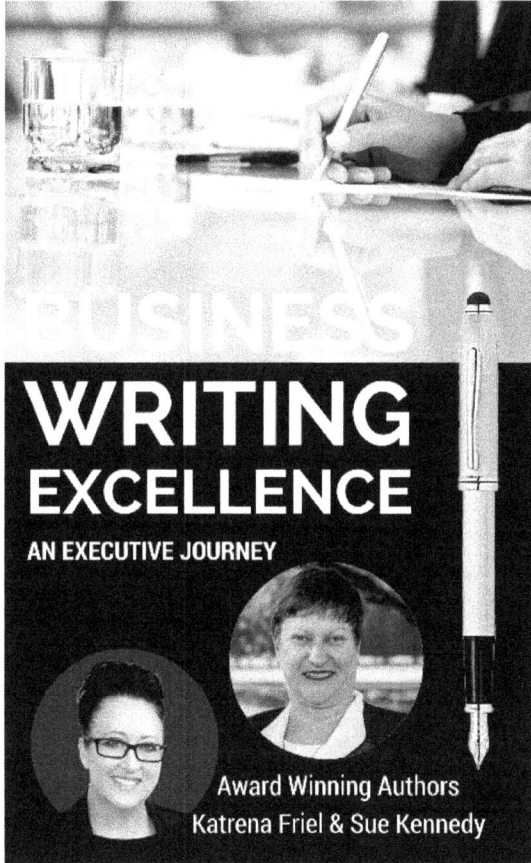

## Business Writing Excellence

The ability to write in a clear and effective way seems to have lost some of the shine and importance as our lives have evolved into a move faster paced way of life, it is now a world where we communicate via text or email.

Don't be misled into believing that this holds true at any corporate level. It is imperative that you develop appropriate written communication skills within your business.

If your communications need to be clear and say exactly what you intend, if they need to have the right tone or inferences, if it needs to effectively sell your ideas or innovations in a manner that engages your target audience, you need to make sure that you are communicating exactly what is intended so you don't let yourself or your company down each time you need to communicate to your audience. This workshop will ensure you get this part of your communication right every single time.

Most executives are 'time poor', they have strict deadlines to meet and many meetings become overwhelming because of this. This workshop is designed to help and guide you into becoming the best minute taker ever and allows you to be able to prepare and take fast and effective notes at your meetings.

## Who Should Attend?

For all those who need to increase their efficiency and effectiveness. This course is designed for all Executives who realise that if they are to be successful and be able to communicate effectively with business leaders at the highest level, they must have the appropriate written communication skills.

## Workshop Agenda

- Personal Learning Objectives (Group Discussion)
- Discover why good writing skills are so important?
- Understand your reader
- Discover the two types of readers
- How to deliver bad news
- The Business of Writing
- Understand how to power write
- Choosing the right medium
- Do's and Don'ts of Business Writing
- Useful Tools and Resources
- Editing & Proofing
- The Art of Minute Writing
- Meetings….the good, the bad and the ugly
- The importance of a well-run meeting
- Understanding roles and responsibilities
- Guidelines to remember

- Meeting Responsibilities checklist
- The 6 Golden rules for Managing a Meeting
- Your Business Writing Checklist
- How to read others – the 4 learning styles
- Locus of Control and Influence
- Learn the Influence Framework
- Learn 8 Expressive Influence Tactics and Behaviours
- Learn 8 Receptive Influence Tactics and Behaviours
- Uncover your Behavioural Style
- Using DISC for Effective Written Communication
- Design your own Personal Development Strategy

## For information and bookings, please call us on 0448 224 287 or email us at sue@allthingswriting.com.au

*All Things Writing*
—— SUE KENNEDY ——